Why I Stay

Why I Stay 2

The Challenges of Discipleship for Contemporary Latter-day Saints

ROBERT A. REES, EDITOR

SIGNATURE BOOKS | 2021 | SALT LAKE CITY

The opinions expressed in this book are not necessarily those of the publisher.

Cover design by Jason Francis.

FIRST EDITION | 2021

LIBRARY OF CONGRESS CATALOGING-IN-PUBLICATION DATA

Why I stay : the challenges of discipleship for contemporary
Mormons / edited by Robert A. Rees.
      p. cm.
      Includes bibliographical references.
      ISBN 978-1-56085-291-9
1. Mormons—Religious life. 2. Church of Jesus Christ of Latter-day
Saints—Membership. I. Rees, Robert A., 1935- editor.
      BX8656.W55 2011
      248.4'893—dc23   2011030893

Contents

Editor's Introduction:
The Sacred Space at the Edge of the Inside

> "If you find any earthly institution that is ten
> percent divine, embrace it with all your heart!"
> —Laurel Thatcher Ulrich, *All God's*
> *Critters Got a Place in the Choir*

The landscape of Mormonism has changed dramatically since the first volume of *Why I Stay* was published in 2011, and that changed landscape introduces both urgency and complexity to the question of why people stay or don't stay in the Church of Jesus Christ of Latter-day Saints. Many who never expected to consider that question have been asking it of themselves—and having it asked of them by others. It is not as simple a question as it once was.

While there are no reliable statistics on what some refer to as "the Mormon faith crisis," there is little doubt that such a crisis exists. One LDS leader characterized it as the most significant faith crises since the time of Kirtland, Ohio, in the 1830s.[1] It is safe to say that more Latter-day Saints than at any other time in the modern church have left, are in the process of leaving, or are contemplating leaving—or, at least, struggling with that question. While there has been no comprehensive scientific study of the Mormon faith crisis to date, informal studies, reports, and signs suggest that it is both real and growing, which makes the expressions of thoughtful, committed faith contained in this collection all the more valuable. Jana Riess's *The Next Mormons*[2] confirms that among Latter-day Saint Millennials "retention is down," but, she adds, "there's an abundance of good news if you're a Mormon leader. Mormons still have the highest rates of marriage in the United States, extremely high self-reported findings about belief in God and religious practices such as daily prayer, and low incidence of high-risk behavior. The bad news is that retention is slipping, and younger generations appear to be leading the way."[3]

What is the nature if the contemporary faith crisis? For the past seven or so years, as I understand, the First Presidency and Quorum of the Twelve have had a document titled "LDS Personal Faith Crisis,"[4] which is the work of a small independent group of engaged Latter-day Saints deeply concerned about the vulnerability of the church to the erosion of both membership and reputation among the general populace. That document lists four primary factors influencing the faith crisis:

Unprecedented access to information
Continual access to information
Unprecedented content creation and consumption
The Mormon Moment

While the "Mormon Moment" (which centered on the 2002 Salt Lake City International Winter Olympics, Proposition 8 in California, Mitt Romney's presidential campaign, and the popularity of *The Book of Mormon* Broadway musical) may have passed, or, at least, diminished, the other factors noted in this report have only grown in influence and significance. That is, the internet and social media have made it possible for nearly every bit of information and every possible point of view about the church and Mormonism to be accessed by millions of people around the world. Another way of putting this is that for the first 170 years of its existence, the church significantly was able to control its own narrative. That is no longer the case. Potentially anyone on the planet with a smartphone has access to nearly everything known about the church, its history, its culture, and its governance, including the unattractive and unsavory aspects contained in that information environment—and including a plethora of myth and misinformation. When the first volume of *Why I Stay* was published in 2011, the Latter-day Saint presence on the internet was blossoming; since then, it has become a garden full of wonderful flowers but also of weeds and abundant *fleurs du mal*—in which multiple gardeners contend for control.

There is also evidence of Latter-day Saint faith strengthening in some areas, which is related to leadership's attempt to create and maintain "Centers of Strength," which consolidate leadership and resources. The church has taken other proactive steps to counter the erosion of membership, including publishing a number of Gospel Topics essays on critical and controversial subjects (see churchofjesuschrist.org/study/manual/gospel-topics-essays/essays). Nevertheless, the church is not immune from its past, its present mistakes and miscalculations, or the effects of a growing secularism in the West, all of which affect the retention of members, not only in the Church of Jesus Christ of Latter-day Saints, but in many faith organizations.

The faith crisis represents not just a failure of faith but also a failure of reason and, especially, a failure of love. Those combined failures have created a situation in which Latter-day Saints are pulled toward opposite ends of the religious spectrum, increasingly divided into camps that tend to see one another as misguided, unrighteous, and even alien. The casualty is the middle ground where dialogue and mutual respect are possible. The polar pull—both in the church and in society in general—away from the more complex, challenging, and uncertain center, tends toward reductionism and oversimplification of both secular and spiritual life.

David Brooks, the *New York Times* columnist, identifies these positions as including those who are at the core, those who are on the outside, and those who are "at the edge of the inside" of an organization. The first tend to be purists and defenders, the second critics and attackers, and the third "people [who] are within the organization, but they're not subsumed by group think. They work at the boundaries, bridges and entranceways." Brooks argues that there is little constructive discourse between insiders and outsiders, each of who tends to demonize the other. Those on the edge of the inside, however, neither idolize those in the center nor demonize those on the outside. Rather they play the role of "partners in a reality that is paradoxical, complementary and unfolding."[5]

Brooks draws on the work of the Franciscan priest Richard Rohr, who argues that those who live on the edge of any group "are free from its central seductions, but also free to hear its core message in very new and creative ways." Rohr sees such people as doorkeepers: "A doorkeeper must love both the inside and the outside of his or her group, and know how to move between these two loves."[6]

Brooks elucidates: "A person at the edge of inside can be the strongest reformer. This person has the loyalty of a faithful insider, but the judgment of the critical outsider. ... A person on the edge of the inside knows how to take advantage of the standards and practices of an organization but not be imprisoned by them."[7] This is similar to the wise advice Juanita Brooks's father gave her at a time in her life when she was questioning the certainty and literalness of scripture and various aspects of her faith. She writes,

> One day Dad said to me, "My girl, if you follow this tendency to criticize, I'm afraid you will talk yourself out of the Church. I'd hate to see you do that. I'm a cowboy, and I've learned that if I ride *in* the herd, I am lost—totally helpless. One who rides counter to it is trampled and killed. One who only trails behind means little, because he leaves all responsibility to others. It is the cowboy who rides the edge of the herd, who sings and calls and makes himself heard who helps direct the course. ... So don't lose yourself, and don't ride away and desert the outfit. Ride the edge of the herd and be alert, but know your directions, and call out loud and clear. Chances are, you won't make any difference, but on the other hand, you just might."[8]

I see the contributors to this collection, as I saw those in the first volume, as Latter-day Saints whose discipleship is magnified from the edge of the inside of Mormonism, "with fear and trembling" (Philip. 2:12), but also with even more love and faith. Their expressions represent a small but influential segment of contemporary Latter-day Saint voices. The writers come from a cross-section of professions (university professors, artists, attorneys, scientists, psychotherapists, entrepreneurs, poets, and others). While not representative of church demographics in general, three—Charles Inouye, Kimberly Applewhite Teitter, and Gloria Pak—represent ethnic minorities, and half are women. Perhaps in the future, those responsible for selecting participants for the "Why I Stay" session of Sunstone will invite more non-Americans, minorities, and those of younger generations to give voice to why they stay.

There are a number of reasons why editing this collection proved to be more challenging than editing the first. Perhaps the most dramatic difference is that not every participant who spoke at the Sunstone Symposium's "Why I Stay" session has indeed stayed in the church, which narrowed the choices available for inclusion in this volume. Some who responded to the invitation to submit essays later withdrew their submissions; others who spoke of staying wrote essays that suggested that at least on some level they weren't planning on staying. Several of the essays were solicited outside the Sunstone Symposium speakers. Nine years ago, when I was editing the first collection, I found my own essay, "I Place It in My Heart," inspired by the expressions of the other contributors to that volume. Those personal reflections, honest introspections, and inspired witnesses of some of the most thoughtful Latter-day Saints of my generation, led me to contemplate what it means to make an ultimate commitment to the restored gospel—and to the church that bears its message to the world. I continue to value both the variety and quality of those essays because they continue to inform and inspire my own commitment and devotion. I feel the same about the essays included in this volume. Together, these voices give evidence of the remarkable legacy of Joseph Smith's religious imagination, his boldness in challenging the religious axioms and institutions of his day, his restoration of ancient ordinances and doctrines, and his addition of new scripture that constitutes the heart of the LDS tradition. Together, these essays demonstrate that the progressive voice is vital to the health of Mormonism. Perhaps not every contributor herein would identify her- or himself as "progressive," but each of these personal expressions fits at least one of the standard definitions of that word: (1) "developing gradually or in stages; proceeding step by step," or (2) "favoring or implementing social reform or new, liberal ideas."[9] Most fit both.

In my judgment, such progressiveness, although representing a minority view within Mormonism, is disproportionally essential to the future of the church and its mission of helping, along with other believers and religious faiths, to redeem the world. The writers are neither blindly nor blithely committed to the church, but are so with eyes and hearts wide open, aware of the issues that cause others to leave, but also aware that a commitment to faith should be able to accommodate human imperfection as well as institutional errancy, ineffectiveness, and inefficiency. These authors recognize that at times all religions, just as all individuals, do unfortunate, hurtful, even transgressive things. Beyond that, their mature discipleship helps them recognize that any ultimate ideal can only be achieved or, at least, approached in and through imperfect people living in an imperfect world.

One of the themes that emerges from these essays is deep compassion for those who are in faith crisis or estranged from the church. That is, unlike the judgment that many lapsed or ex-Mormons experience from family, leaders, and fellow members, these writers, having wrestled with many of the same issues that lead some to leave, take a broader perspective. As Curt Bench says, succinctly, "I look at the church as I do family (both of which can sometimes be dysfunctional): I don't always *like* my family members, but I always *love* them. I don't like everything about the church, but I love the church and its members."

Most, if not all, of the contributors to this volume have encountered leaders and fellow members who wonder why they stay, with the implication that both they and the church would be better off if they didn't stay. I love Susan Hinckley's response to such sentiments: "I've imagined being asked from the smug seats in the middle of the chapel or—on the worst Sundays—from behind the pulpit, the question aimed at my chair in the overflow. Why don't you leave? Anyone can see you're in the process of leaving—you've been complaining, disagreeing, and uncomfortable for as long as we've know each other—*why don't you leave?* My answer is that if someone assumes I'm in the process of leaving, they have misunderstood me. I am in the process of staying."

Most of the contributors choose to stay as active, devoted, tithe-paying, temple-attending members, and find joy in doing so. As Jody England writes, "I stay because of the temple. Each time I go, I take on someone's name, and for a short while, I become them. Their concerns are mine, and I think mine can become theirs. I experience at-one-ment with those who live throughout time and distance, and I learn to love, through them, all people as my brothers and sisters." Parker Blount, on the other hand, prefers a more distant relationship with the church, which he declares is nevertheless nearly always in his consciousness: "If you have been engaged with the church for a sufficient time, there is a point where the church, as part of your psyche, doesn't leave you alone. At least daily something about the church enters into the chatter of my thoughts. There are times when I deliberately invite them in. But there are other times I can have an idea that I wish to pursue, and I sit down to make some notes about it, and the next thing I know it has morphed into something about the church. I didn't intend to write about the church; I wanted to stay away from it, but there it comes like mist rising off the river. In that sense the church simply abides with me, is my ever-present companion."

Eric Samuelson, the late distinguished Mormon playwright who suffered opprobrium and rejection because of his boldness in dramatizing the complexity of contemporary Latter-day Saint life, acknowledges that such experiences cause some to leave the faith. Nevertheless, he offers a simple declaration of his devotion: "I am a Mormon because I was raised in a Mormon family. I grew up going to church every Sunday, attending Primary and MIA. When I turned nineteen, I went on a mission to Norway. Why have I stayed? Because it has never occurred to me to leave."

Emma Lou Thayne, who, like Samuelson, passed away after this project was begun, acknowledges some changes in her faith over time, but considers them expansive to her faith: "Through allegiance, affinity, and affection, the pillars of my faith are still intact, and, yes, the roof has blown blessedly off the structure to reveal a whole sky full of stars. I wonder what the next years of the counseling of life might have to say about why I stay both here and then there. Negative only now and then, that wondering. I can hardly wait to see."

Sometimes staying comes down to particular circumstances of seeing Christ's gospel work in one's life or family. Kathleen Cattani recounts such an experience: "During the last month of my father's life, the men from his High Priest's quorum took turns staying with him at night so that we could sleep. One of these brothers was with my father when he died early one morning. The members of our ward brought to life the words in Mosiah about those who are willing to bear one another's burdens and to mourn with those that mourn, and comfort those that stand in need of comfort (Mosiah 18:8–10)."

As a scientist, Alan Eastman compares his faith to understanding thermodynamics: "All of this reminds me of a comment from the professor with whom I studied advanced thermodynamics: 'The first time I took thermodynamics, I hardly understood anything. The second time, I took thermodynamics, I thought I understood all but a few little details. The third time I took thermodynamics, I realized I didn't understand it at all, but by then it was so useful that I couldn't do anything without it.' As with science, I've come to realize that I don't understand spiritual things at all well, but they are so dear to me now that I refuse do to without them. When it comes right down to it, that's why I stay."

Instead of writing about *why* he stays, Mitch Mayne, an active, openly gay Latter-day Saint focuses on *how* he stays, including, keeping a clear distinction between his commitment to the church and his commitment to Christ: "Placing my faith in the institution instead of in Christ is a bit like putting my faith in the sales team and not the product. By recognizing and placing faith in my Savior—where it rightly belongs—I have allowed myself to let go of many unrealistic expectations I once had of my religion. And, as a friend once told me, an expectation is nothing more than a premeditated resentment."

After raising and then responding to a series of provocative questions, Phil Barlow concludes, "The choice to remain or to leave the fold is not merely a product of reason or of belief. Our choices also entail emotion, intuition, 'spirit,' relationships, commitments, values, and habits of character. I have found these elements conspire to enrich my Mormon life, to orient it toward noble aspirations and meaning, to afford a fine workshop for service and soul-making. I may be an idiosyncratic Saint. Certainly, I am a flawed one. But I thrive in the Mormon way."

Ronda Roberts-Callister examines her LDS life in relation to both *utility* (with the focus on usefulness) and *validity* (with the focus on truth) and concludes, "As soon as I understood the distinction between the two, I immediately recognized that I fall on the side of utility. I have found over time that specific beliefs matter much less to me than an overarching framework of how I live my life. … When I consider why I stay, my primary question is, 'Is the church helping me to become a better person?' Feeling that it does explains why I choose to stay."

This is similar to the reasons given by Jennifer Finlayson-Fife: "I have found the courage to stay and invest in my religious community because of my confidence that creating the body of Christ is not a top-down endeavor and not an exclusively obedience-driven endeavor. Instead, in creating the body of Christ, a godly people is forged through communal striving to live according to earnestly sought truth and to love one another. This ideal gives me confidence to learn from others, including leaders, and then stand for what I honestly believe. It gives me courage to invest in my Mormon people. I want to live up to the best in Mormonism and stand for the goodness in it and not allow false traditions to be given gospel status. I am grateful for all that this community of believers has given to me, and I choose to stay in the moral conversation and invest in return. This is why I stay."

Carol Lynn Pearson expresses a similar sentiment in a powerful epigrammatic statement: "There are two very large reasons [why I stay]. One—I find a great deal of love in this church. Two—where I do not find love, I have an opportunity to help create love." In contrast to Carol Lynn's simple declaration is Russell Frandsen's expansive list of "Thirty-Two Variations on an Enduring Theme," a compendium of spiritual, experiential, and rational reasons for his enduring commitment to stay in the church.

I am pleased this collection includes essays from minority groups who represent the increasing diversity of Christ's kingdom as well as Mormonism's particular expressions of it. What these essays suggest is that North American members of the church especially have much to learn from other cultures, other races, other traditions, and other voices. A beautiful example is Charles Inouye's essay, "The Lasting Pain of Thankfulness," which draws a parallel between Zen and Zion, between the repetitive diurnal practices of Buddhism and Mormonism. Inouye refers to these practices as "raking," a metaphor from his forthcoming memoir, *Zion Earth Zen Sky—Learning to Rake*. He says, "Given the possibility of getting over my delusional notion of self, what actually saves me is what I call raking, this disciplined way of attending to the same practical tasks day after day, week after week, year after year. … The genius of Zen is the genius of Mormonism. Both bring the abstract concepts of heaven down to earth. Both make the ordinary things of this world the way to salvation. Our precise garden is made of imprecise sand. And so we have to get out there and rank and rake. … What we can learn from this constant raking is a simply yet salutary lesson: doing something repeatedly can be the opposite of boring. In fact, it might be the best way to avoid ennui, anomie, alienation, nihilism, and so on. This way of loyalty and dedication makes everything in our lives a manifestation of god's love and goodness—even when we're making mistakes."

Gloria Pak speaks of integrating her ethnic Korean culture with her religious culture: "I stay to live into the question of how to integrate my roots. There is a temptation to start from scratch and leave behind all that is familiar, but that doesn't feel right. So that question burns right. Whether it is my Korean heritage or my religious heritage, I recognize there are unique gifts in each tradition, and I am exploring how to preserve those gifts while letting go of the constructs that no longer serve us or future generations. In some circles they call this the ability to transcend and include, leaving nothing good behind as we mature."

As this collection was being prepared for press, the United States, and indeed the entire world, was going through the birth pangs of a social and political revolution sparked by the brutal killing of George Floyd, a Black man from Minneapolis. His death was the proverbial tip of the iceberg that opened the floodgates (which, given climate change, may turn out not to be a mixed metaphor!) of racial and social injustice. This coincided with the publication of Joanna Brooks's, *Mormonism and White Supremacy: American Religion and the Problem of White Innocence* (Oxford, 2020), which awakened the unfinished dialogue about racism within the Church of Jesus Christ of Latter-day Saints. Kimberly Applewhite Teitter's essay herein, "Lessons from My Grandma's House," is a powerful and poignant witness of the treacherous terrain a Black female Latter-day Saint in an interracial marriage has had to negotiate. She concludes, "I suppose that to answer the question of why I stay, I could have succinctly said this: as I have stayed with God, God has stayed with me, and staying in the church has allowed me to see him stay in the spiritual language I know best. ... If I had not stayed, I would not be able to see where God has brought me. ... I would not be able to see how God has never left me, even when I felt at times like everyone and every other group had."

The beauty of these essays is that they stimulate one to think as well as to believe. This is what Dan Wotherspoon does in his essay, "Called to Grow the Kingdom," by posing the question: Is it by God's design that we find such a diversity of religious truths, traditions, and spiritual practices in the world? He concludes that God wants every truth "to be as loved as much as possible, to be as deeply explored as humanly possible, to be presented and defended and put into the ongoing human experience as much as possible … to be lived, explored deeply from the inside, and examined in comparison with others." He concludes, "I believe it is truly an act of love that God doesn't have us be [i.e., practice] all religions at once, as we'd fail at that. It is an act of love by God to the truths themselves (and hence to the world) to allow, even encourage, deep, soulful commitment to very particular truths while at the same time making it possible for us, as we grow spiritually, to glean from other faiths truths that complement and expand our own."

A related view is expressed in Camilla Miner Smith's essay: "The problem with tribalism comes when we only look to the inside of the circle, facing inward rather than using the strength of that circle to face outward to the larger world where we can bless others. The Jews have a Hebrew term for this concept: *Tikkun olam,* repairing the world." This is a beautiful idea, just as it is beautiful that God makes possible for Latter-day Saints in all our diversity to expand the borders of Zion through the gift of his Son, the inspiration and guidance of the Holy Spirit, and the rich revelations and lived experience found in the restored gospel. That richness is evident in these expressions of commitment, constancy, dedication, devotion, and love.

One of the contributors who withdrew her essay from this collection, because of the church's policy on same-sex married couples and their children, gave me permission to quote from her essay. I was deeply touched by what she had written, including her reference to a wonderful poem by Phillip Larkin titled "Church Going." In the poem, the speaker stops at a parish church in rural England. It is clear that he is no longer a believer and regards the church almost as an anthropologist would, examining and contemplating various artifacts:

> matting seats and stone
> and little books; sprawlings of flowers cut
> For Sunday brownish now; some brass and stuff
> Up at the holy end; the small neat organ;
> And a tense musty unignorable silence …

He concludes that "the place was not worth stopping for," but quickly adds,

> Yet stop I did: in fact I often do
> And always end much at a loss like this
> Wondering what to look for; wondering too

When churches fall completely out of use
What we shall turn them into …

And then he asks the ultimate question:

And what remains when disbelief has gone?

What indeed? His observations on the decay and death of this particular church ("A shape less recognisable each week") symbolize what he sees as the decay and death of belief itself. And yet, in leaving the church, he says, "It pleases me to stand in silence here, / A serious house on serious earth." The lovely essay I wish I could have included in this collection ended with the following poignant statement by the author, who has now chosen not to stay, or to stay on her terms, which makes me mourn even more that this good woman no longer finds herself in a Latter-day Saints church on Sundays:

I stay because, most Sundays, I find myself in a serious house on serious earth, where my most important compulsions meet and are robed as destinies. Since I am forever surprising a hunger in myself to be more serious, I find I gravitate with it to this ground, my ward, the small, rich world which, for me, has become the church.

What a loss of such a bright, sensitive Latter-day Saint! Hopefully, those of us who remain in our (sometimes) serious houses of worship will work to welcome her—and all the others who have left—back home, home to the inside, even, or perhaps especially, if it is the edge of that inside.

Notes

1. "And they [church leaders] realize that, maybe, since Kirtland we've never had a period of—I'll call it apostasy—like we're having right now, largely over these issues." Remarks by Elder Marlin Jensen on November 11, 2013, at a forum at Utah State University. For a transcript of and commentary on the exchange, see www.fairmormon.org/blog/2013/01/15/reports-of-the-death-of-the-church-are-greatly-exaggerated.

2. *The Next Mormons: How Millennials Are Changing the LDS Church* (New York: Oxford University Press, 2019).

3. At www.religionnews.com/2016/04/14/mormons-20s-30s-leaving-lds-church.

4. While the document referred to, "LDS Personal Faith Crisis," reveals that the Mormon faith crisis cuts across many demographics (age, gender, education, income, length of church activity, etc.), more recent evidence, including that in Riess's *The Next Mormons,* suggests that the problem is more critical among young, single members. Whatever the evidence, coupled with the church's gradual decline in growth in 2018, the growth rate in the United States of 0.6 percent was half the international rate of 1.2 percent—although there was a countervailing increase in activity, with 400 more congregations than in the previous year.

5. At www.nytimes.com/2016/06/24/opinion/at-the-edge-of-inside.html.

6. As quoted by Brooks, at www.nytimes.com/2016/06/24/opinion/at-the-edge-of-inside.html.

7. Brooks, at www.nytimes.com/2016/06/24/opinion/at-the-edge-of-inside.html.

8. Davis Bitton and Maureen Ursenbach, "Riding Herd: A Conversation with Juanita Brooks," *Dialogue: A Journal of Mormon Thought* 9, 1 (Spring 1974): 12.

9. At www.en.oxforddictionaries.com/definition/us/progressive.

Why I Stay

R. A. Christmas

Another faith-promoting chiasmus!

Because if I left the church my wife'd kill me—
  and who knows, polygamy might come back!
    Besides, I've been a Mormon for so long
     I can't even imagine not being one.
      And, finally and frankly, I stay because
      I have a testimony of the Restored Gospel;
       I know God lives; Jesus is the Christ;
        the Book of Mormon is the Word of God.
        The Prophet Joseph Smith translated
       the Book of Mormon by the power of God,
      saw and spoke with the Father and the Son.
     The Holy Ghost tells me these things are true.
    And let me end by saying, in all sincerity,
   that if, by chance, I were to leave the church,
  after having been a member for almost sixty years,
 and then, say, polygamy happened to come back—
for sure I'd be begging my (one) wife to shoot me!

Questing and Questioning

Philip L. Barlow

I have before me a series of letters a private elementary school teacher reportedly assigned her students to address to God. The letters pose questions.

Here is one by a girl named Jennifer:

Dear God,
    Did you *mean* for the ostrich to look like that?

This one is from David:

Dear God,
    Instead of letting people die and having to make new ones, why don't you just keep the ones you have now?

And this from Megan:

Dear God,
    Thank you for the baby brother. But what I prayed for was a puppy.

The issues behind such innocent queries eventually ripen. In adults, they may take the form of protest—against the injustices of the world, against the implausibility of things, against the universe itself. Such protests warrant attention; they range as broadly as humanity and often morph into anger towards or rejection of God and contempt for or indifference towards religion. "God-rage" goes back at least as far as the ancient Sumerian *Epic of Gilgamesh,* one of humankind's oldest and most enduring tales—older by a millennium or more than Homer or the Hebrew Bible (at least, in the form that we have the Bible today).[1]

Protest against the gods was widespread as well in ancient Greece. It also is manifest in many biblical passages: "Why do the wicked prosper?" asks Jeremiah. "I want a hearing!" demands Job. "God has set us a heavy and futile task," observes the philosopher-author of Ecclesiastes. Even the Christ asks, "Why have you forsaken me?" as he hangs impaled on his cross. Humans sometimes find their gods inconvenient, questionable, even inscrutable.

Is it God alone, however, who needs to be questioned? Or, as is implicit in the children's letters above, is it also ourselves—our expectations and presumptions?

In the natural world, we come to know wonder, awe, delight, and an awareness of our own contingency. At least, we do unless we allow these native urges to be dulled by fatigue, distractions, bustle, bad teaching, hormones, and who-knows-what? We experience the amazing capacity to contemplate ourselves and a sense of right and wrong that eclipses cultural particularities. We may feel beckoned by a power beyond ourselves and toward something higher, finer, and filled with enduring meaning. Perhaps we glimpse the "giftedness" of all things, the grace behind existence. These are seeds of the religious impulse.

Alas, we also know pain. We encounter it, read about it, watch it on television and in the cinema. Some suffering seems beyond rational justification. Despite auxiliary causes, a world history soaked to its core in blood and heartbreak is the spine of traditional atheism, certainly in Western civilization.

This conflicting combination of awe and questing, on the one hand, and woe and horror, on the other, can be so potent as to separate us from ourselves and from God. The contradiction may even lead some to say, as I recall having read somewhere, but cannot now confirm, that Voltaire allegedly did: "To believe in God is impossible; not to believe ... is absurd."

All this is, of course, too large to reckon with in short compass. Before turning to the specific concerns of Mormonism, however, permit me two observations. The first is to acknowledge that there is an element of choice in my faith, notwithstanding all prayer, spiritual intuition, and reasoning. A broad existential contradiction looms in sensing that there is something or someone to which we are responsible who is higher and beyond the reality we know—and yet who at the same time reigns over a tormented creation without making things clearer and more palatable to us. This two-pronged problem confronts not only Latter-day Saints and other religious people; it is a problem posed to all human beings. Skepticism or indifference, no less than belief, are matters of choice—ones with intellectual difficulties of their own.

The second observation notes that while untenable suffering is the most influential reason for discarding religion, it also is the seed bed for the rise of religion itself. Comprehending the first premise of Buddhism (commonly though inadequately rendered as "life is suffering") is, for devotees, the initial step toward "enlightenment." Islam gained traction in the seventh century in part because Muhammad encountered a society he found corrupt, oppressive, dysfunctional, and in need of inspired reconstruction. Despite homage given to the account of Creation and to the figure of Abraham, the Hebrew consciousness as a historically traceable entity began more securely with the Exodus, Israel's paradigmatic event, wherein a people came to believe that God had entered history to lead them away from centuries of degradation and bondage and into a new life and peoplehood bound by covenant. As far as we can determine through the tools of history and literary criticism, Christian consciousness did not begin in a picturesque manger so much as on a wretched cross, along with Christ's disciples' subsequent reflections about what that event and its conquest meant in conjunction with their Lord's earlier teachings.

In short, critics cannot successfully dismiss religion on the grounds that there is horrendous suffering in the world and with the presumption that a good God would not allow it, for suffering contributes to why religion arises in the first place. It is possible to construe religion fundamentally as *response*—diagnosis of and response to the world's suffering.

Within such wider contexts as these, I remain a Latter-day Saint because I find in the church an extraordinary social and personal resource for responding to such existential questions about the nature of the world. The Restoration ushered into the world by Joseph Smith proffers assistance for the pursuit of the good, the true, and the beautiful—it is an aide in the quest for what is meaningful, enduring, and loving. The gospel and the supporting structure of the church provide a marvelous laboratory of practical action for those seeking states of mind and soul and relations and futures worthy of aspiration. Why would I ever forfeit such a resource? Why would I abandon a people exquisitely organized to help relieve suffering, to foster self-improvement, to serve, and to seek righteousness and the things that matter most?

In truth, I have considered stepping back from the church at two junctures in my life: once in relation to philosophical and historical matters I encountered while working toward a doctorate in the study of religion and history, and again as I was troubled about certain church policies and practices and what I considered the ill-advised and deplorable treatment of certain individuals by church officials. These were for me substantive matters, not to be ignored. What follows suggests why these problems do not compel me to abandon the LDS virtues, understandings, and the fellowship I find distinctive and admirable.

Shall I abandon Mormonism because I discover problems in the life of Joseph Smith and LDS history generally? Along with published scholarship, formal education, independent pondering by diverse individuals, and word-of-mouth networks, the internet (sometimes responsibly, sometimes not) has introduced questions about such matters to a wider circle than formerly. My perspective in addressing these problems allows me to retain my faith. Many believers construe the church to be essentially divine, marred only by the minor imperfections of a few well-meaning leaders or by outright sinners or those who suffer from a lack of faith. All significant decisions at church headquarters and all church publications are, in this view, inspired and right. By contrast, I construe the church to be made up *entirely* of human beings, from Joseph Smith onward—with all of the implications that view implies. These generally admirable people are not immune from human failings: selfishness, self-promotion, limited understanding, insensitivity, authoritarianism, defensiveness, sexism, racism, homophobia, or anti-intellectualism, for example. It helps me to remember that the church at every level is made up entirely of imperfect people, like me, who are trying to respond to the divine with which they have (in faith) been touched. This formula spares me the temptation to suspend critical thinking in the face of thorny issues of history or church policy. It also calls forth my charity, humility, and loyalty. I *assume* weakness, error, and limited understanding to abound in all of us, and I am delighted and humbled as I work with those who aspire to be saints and when I discover inspired strands that invite us to something higher.

Ought I feel betrayed when I learn of historical problems to which

I should have been exposed in the course of growing up in the church? I can sympathize with those who do feel betrayed. I used to be startled when I encountered in my college classes students who were disturbed to learn basic facts of Mormon history: aspects of Joseph Smith's practice of polygamy, perhaps, or that racism was common in an earlier Mormonism as it was in society at large. "Why wasn't I told this earlier?" "What else wasn't I told?"—they ask. This launches some on a search, variously fueled by legitimate or sensationalized questions, by honest inquiry or by manic anger.

I also sympathize with church leaders who want church meetings to be spiritual and inspiring and thus do not focus on problems. In general, their intent is not to deceive but to edify, and many who have prepared inadequate church curricula over the years, to say nothing of the lay teachers who enact the resulting manuals, have been earnest but not historically well-grounded. So I am not sure that a sense of conscious "betrayal" is in many cases the most apt response. But, yes, we need as a church to address this issue. After an aborted effort in the 1970s, the Historical Department of the Church has since the late 1990s been at the forefront of promoting a more conversant and honest rendering of Mormonism's history, with its challenges and its glories. Augmenting that, we need to do a better job with the quality of our curricula and manuals as a whole, which can be done in an informed, honest, and faith-promoting way. Overall, I judge the history and practice of the Restoraion to be remarkable, defensible, and often inspiring.

Shall I leave because I wince at how commonly my people rehearse to themselves that we are God's uniquely chosen people? I am not leaving, but I do wince. Prayer, study, and experience lead me to conclude that we Saints are a people *among* God's peoples. Latter-day Saints are not necessarily chosen because of inherent moral and spiritual superiority. We tell ourselves otherwise often enough, citing the Book of Abraham (3:23ff) while perhaps assuming that the pre-existent "great and noble ones" are largely the Latter-day Saints. Jesus, however, challenged such attitudes among the "chosen people" of his time. "'We have Abraham as our father,' you tell me. But I tell you that out of these stones God can raise up children for Abraham" (Matt. 3:9). Nephi similarly targeted elitist presumption: "Know ye not that there are more nations than one? Know ye not that I, the Lord your God, have created all men, and that I remember those who are upon the isles of the sea; and that I rule in the heavens above and in the earth beneath; and I bring forth my word unto the children of men, yea, even upon all the nations of the earth?" (2 Ne. 29:7).

If we are indeed a chosen people, we need not presume our superiority. Rather, we are a people tasked with a commission. We have *good news* and good ways to share. This, however, does not preclude the Lord from commissioning others in their own roles. The God of heaven and earth is not so small as any number of clans have presumed.

The church is not the only source of that which is good, true, and beautiful—after which we are invited to seek. If I believed it was, I should quickly run into two problems. The first is experience—experience with people outside my LDS faith, contemporarily and across history, who regularly enlighten me with their wisdom and goodness. The second problem is that such a misconception would introduce not merely paradox but contradiction into my faith. Joseph Smith recorded in 1831 a subsequently canonized statement that the newly formed "Church of Christ" was "the only true and living church upon the face of the whole earth, with which I, the Lord, am well pleased" (D&C 1:30), however we are to interpret that. Certainly this comported with Joseph's early understanding that an apostasy had occurred in Christianity, that the traditional creeds did not please Joseph's God, and that a new authority was necessary to carry out the commission that was laid on the new church's shoulders. Yet the same prophet also declared in his later years that one of the "grand fundamental principles of Mormonism" is to seek, from any source, that which is true, virtuous, lovely, or of good report. And I encounter these good elements all around me. It is not merely that other churches have "partial truths" that may be supplemented, which is commonly acknowledged among Latter-day Saints. It is also that I have much to learn and garner from them. Apparently the mature Joseph Smith did not find such teachings a threat to his proclamation of a "restoration" of truths, authority, and open-ended revelation.[2]

Am I disenchanted by LDS proclamations to be the one authentic restoration of original Christianity even though historical study reveals differences in the beliefs, practices, and organization of the first-century church and in the more ancient Israel? Not in any way that prompts me to a loss of faith. For one thing, Joseph Smith rapidly grew and evolved in his understanding. He eventually used the term "restoration" in several distinct senses. The most popularly understood is the recovery of that which is lost: truths, practices, scriptures, or authorities no longer extant because of apostasy or because of evolving institutional needs and understanding (as may also be traced in the history of the modern church itself—such as the disappearance of the office of church patriarch). A second sense of Smith's "restoration" is the mending of that which is broken, that which is not right. A third sense of the word is the completion of that which is partial: the "restoration" of things "kept hidden from before the foundation of the world." Today the Latter-day Saints innocently use the term "restoration" in various ways that can fit into all three of these spheres, but if they fail to recognize the distinctions they may run aground when some biblical critic argues, for instance, that the historical Jesus did not personally organize a church.

Shall I exit the church because anti-intellectualism persists in the culture? Disregard for the intellect, though lamentably common in our culture that values revelation, is not intrinsic to Mormonism. Moreover, while it is scarcely possible to think too clearly or be too informed, it *is* possible to think in excess or to grow entangled in minutiae. A student can overthink and get lost while cramming for a major exam; a pianist may overthink and diminish her performance. It is possible also to misconstrue "reason" as the only form of intelligence—the result of which, carried to its logical extreme, might produce a better android than a human being. So the *meaning* of intelligence requires discussion, and its uses demand adroit and contextualized application.

Far from anti-intellectual, my religious tradition's founder saw intelligence as central to our being and destiny. His revelations assert that our very essence is intelligence; we are intelligences fully as much as we are spirits, and were both before our birth. Learning has lasting significance because "whatever principle of intelligence we attain unto in this life" will follow us in the hereafter (D&C 130:18). God also is an intelligence, the greatest intelligence of all. If those who value the intellect suppress "the spirit" in unrestrained, rationalized, intellectual inquiry, our relation to divine purpose may fall askew. Yet if, in the interest of alleged spirituality, we repress the intellect, we erode both ourselves and our feel for Joseph Smith's teachings. His notions of exaltation regarded body, mind, and spirit. Our manuals and church curricula need to deepen their quality and inspire genuine probing, growth, and adult information and conversation, though this is not as easy as it might appear in a lay church that intends to remain "one church" while spreading to diverse areas of the world.

Do I find individual freedom constricted within the modern church? Certainly there are cultural and policy bounds and currents to navigate, just as in the worlds of business, education, or community relations so as to enact loyalty, minimize giving offense, and expand constructive action. I am free, however, to believe as I believe and to act as I judge best. I find it helps to distinguish among notions of freedom. One primary distinction divides freedom *from* (rules, obligations, or dangers, perhaps) and freedom *to* (act or achieve something). I may imagine that what I want is freedom *from* rules or obligations, but, in its healthy expression, the church assists us in engaging the freedom *to* become what we need to be for others and for eternal joy. Only through sacrifice and discipline of lesser freedoms are we able to become the most free expression of ourselves—just as high-performing athletes are free to become the best version of themselves only through strict control of their impulses, time, talents, diet, and training. Furthermore, adherence to church strictures, as with athletic or musical participation, is voluntary; we are free likewise to choose another, less disciplined path.

Ought I rebel against authoritarianism sometimes found in the church? The problem does occur at times, as Joseph Smith observed when noting that authority intrinsically risks breeding "unrighteous dominion." And where impure dominion arises, priesthood ends. The powers of heaven, he said,

> cannot be controlled nor handled only upon the principles of righteousness. ... [W]hen we undertake ... to exercise control or dominion or compulsion upon the souls of the children of men, in any degree of unrighteousness ... the heavens withdraw themselves; the Spirit of the Lord is grieved; and ... Amen to ... the authority of that man. ... No power or influence can or ought to be maintained by virtue of the priesthood, only by persuasion, by long-suffering, by gentleness and meekness, and by love unfeigned. (D&C 121:36–41)

There are times to say "No" when authority is abused, as Joseph implied and as occasional incidents in our history (such as the nineteenth-century massacre at Mountain Meadows, Utah) demonstrate. But that does not render authority implicitly evil. Authority and loyalty to that authority enable coordinated action in good causes that is far more potent than in circles that demand scant sacrifice and responsibility to a wider group and to God.

Might I quit attending church because the meetings are often boring? Private complaints on this front are not uncommon in the modern church, and the problem costs us active members of all ages. Many lament what they find to be bland, overly correlated manuals for instruction. Sunday discussions are too often "scripted" in the sense that productive thought is stifled and simplistic answers are presupposed by rhetorical questions and sometimes thin topics.

On the other hand, the issue is trickier than it may seem to many church members where the faith is well-established. The church grows most rapidly in international settings where the members range widely in education and resources. How to reach new converts in such settings, while not condescending to long-term members as children, while yet remaining a coherent single church? And what would alternative methods actually produce in a church where lay members teach one another? Any time spent searching the internet for LDS-related themes reveals not only veins of thoughtful faith and discussion, but a world awash with amateur eggheads ready to beat their drum astride individual hobby horses, asking questions of dubious merit that lead to thickets of esoteric speculation, and even division. I trust we would not, as a church, prefer our Sunday instruction to resemble raucous sessions of the British parliament or the intellectual and political preening available on any number of online commentaries.

As a church, we have over-corrected for such dangers and can do better than we are doing to grow deep, thoughtful spiritual roots. This will require prayer, thought, patience, consultation, a search for better models, a willingness to imagine and experiment, and respect for the needs of the worldwide church. We need better to distinguish between the good principle of achieving a thoughtful simplicity in devotional settings and the counterfeit practice of fostering simple-mindedness. As individuals, we need to remember that our attitudes shape the lens by which we see the world and engage any gospel conversation. Faithful and honest inquiry into gospel fundamentals nourishes the soul; intellectual posturing that strays too far from the gospel's good news does not. Our lack of imagination and preparation in our classes can be poor, but so also can a descent into judgmental attitudes toward people who may be, in our lay church structure, doing their best. Do we personally bother to consider a Sunday lesson ahead of time and construct meaningful lines of inquiry to contribute to class discussions? The basics of the gospel are profound, not trivial; they demand our hearts, might, minds, and strength.

If I don't *know* the church is true "beyond a shadow of a doubt" in the way that many believers profess, shall I admit my doubt forthrightly and depart from the church to retain integrity? Such a move would forfeit many virtues and blessings of active membership, and I see no reason to leave on these grounds. For one thing, questions and doubts are not sins. They are (if not tainted by cynicism, cowardice, or delight in disturbing others' faith) intrinsic to epistemic humility, to thinking and learning, and in some ways to spiritual growth, for our preconceptions frequently need to be questioned or reconfigured. Room for doubt is a natural context for human existence and a thriving faith. For another thing, to "know" means different things to different seekers. Even for those who believe in revelation, we humans at best "see through a glass darkly." We do not have access to ultimate reality; instead we may choose to trust in it. The Hebrew word commonly translated as "to know" in the Bible carries the sense not merely of "to apprehend," but also "to encounter." When I "know" in the context of faith, I refer not merely to an intellectual act or personal inspiration; I speak of my experience.

Over recent generations we Latter-day Saints have seemed to let a single passage in the Book of Mormon dominate our sense of how we know spiritual truth. Moroni 10:4 famously reads: "And when ye shall receive these things, I would exhort you that ye would ask God, the Eternal Father, in the name of Christ, if these things are not true; and if ye shall ask with a sincere heart, with real intent, having faith in Christ, he will manifest the truth of it unto you, by the power of the Holy Ghost." But the passage makes no mention of *how* nor *when* such a manifestation might occur, nor in what fashion. The scriptures in fact propose a range of ways that seekers may "know" spiritual truths. Alma, for example, instructs that spiritual learning may be conducted as an experiment and as a series of deductions, which leads to personal experience at once informed by, and productive of, faith (Alma 32:12–20). Matthew recounts Jesus teaching that the works of the righteous will reveal the truthfulness of the principles they live by (7:16). John portrays Jesus answering his critics thus: "My doctrine is not mine, but his that sent me. If any man will do his will, he shall know of the doctrine, whether it be of God, or whether I speak of myself" (7:16–17). Joseph Smith taught that good doctrine "tastes" good—one can respond to it intuitively. Paul asserted that different gifts of the spirit are dispersed to various disciples, and Joseph Smith elaborated: some are given to know things of the Spirit directly while others are given the gift of believing on their words. Hence spiritual "knowing" is not a monolithic process, and what is meant by "knowing" requires some thought and experience.

Faith is that upon which a person relies; it is the most fundamental trust that a person has, whether she is conscious of it or not. People who trust in nothing do not get out of bed at all. The secularist, the atheist, the Buddhist, the Presbyterian, and the Latter-day Saint all depend on *something* they trust as their foundation—else they cannot function in the world.

The choice to remain or to leave the fold is not only a product of reason or of belief. Our choices also entail emotion, intuition, "spirit," relationships, commitments, values, and habits of character and behavior. I have found these elements conspire to enrich my spiritual life and my life as a whole. They orient it toward noble aspirations and meaning. They afford a fine workshop for service and soul-making.

I may be an idiosyncratic Saint. Certainly I am a flawed one. But I thrive in the Mormon way.

Notes

1. Anonymous, *The Epic of Gilgamesh: An English Version with an Introduction*, rev., trans. N. K. Sandars (New York: Penguin Classics, 1960).

2. On Smith's growth and evolution, see his sermons of July 9 and 16, 1843, less than a year prior to his death, in Andrew F. Ehat and Lyndon

W. Cook, eds., *The Words of Joseph Smith: The Contemporary Accounts of the Nauvoo Discourses of the Prophet Joseph Smith* (Provo, Utah: BYU Religious Studies Center, 1980). For an analysis and context of Smith's "Reformation" of the movement he founded, see Don Bradley, "The Grand Fundamental Principles of Mormonism: Joseph Smith's Unfinished Reformation," *Sunstone*, Apr. 2006, 32–42. A more readily accessible statement implying Mormon readiness to learn from others is the summative statement now canonized as the 13th Article of Faith.

Circles of Light

Susan Hinckley

"You're a good person," my psychiatrist once told me. "You're just not a very good *Mormon*." I couldn't be offended because I knew immediately he was right. It was hard to hear, but it explained a lot. In fact, his observation suddenly seemed like something I'd known for a long time.

I'm naturally rebellious, for one thing. I love questions much more than I want answers. And I'm a raging non-conformist. Tell me what I have to do, wear, say, or believe, and my first reaction is always going to be, "Make me."

I'm pretty sure all of this is in the genes somewhere. Recently an extremely willful daughter confided, "I don't know why I'm this way. But I ask the waiter for his recommendations, and no matter how good he makes the thing sound or how much I want it, I can't order it. Because I'm not going to let anyone tell me what to do." I understand just how she feels.

I believe my psychiatrist meant to make me feel better with his diagnostic aside, and I guess I felt a small validation in it. But it also makes me wonder why I've spent the thirty years since he said it showing up every Sunday, sitting reverently and quietly, singing my beloved hymns with real sincerity, holding callings and performing them reliably, carrying a temple recommend that should reassure me I'm handling the checklist about as well as anyone else, yet still feel that somehow deep inside, programmed by design into my most original equipment, I'm not a good Mormon (at least by some people's standards).

Why continue to be one? It's a question I've been thinking about from the moment I was old enough to realize I have a choice, which makes me think there might be something to the ongoing exercise of figuring it out.

I've imagined being asked from the smug seats in the middle of the chapel or—on the worst Sundays—from behind the pulpit, the question aimed at my chair in the overflow. Why don't you leave? Anyone can see you're in the process of leaving—you've been complaining, disagreeing, and uncomfortable for as long as we've known each other—*Why don't you leave?*

My answer is that if someone assumes I'm in the process of leaving, they have misunderstood me. I am in the process of staying.

I had a lonely childhood for many reasons, none of which are important here, but one image from it is. Sometimes at night, when the house was dark and quiet and I felt most alone, I would look down from my high window at the streetlight that stood directly across from our house. It was always there, standing bravely, fending off the darkness in a circle of light it had to draw for itself on the sidewalk. It never faltered; it stood in the dead of winter, crusted with snow and ice—and in summer, too, coming on magically just as the last long rays of sunlight disappeared at the end of our street. Rather than living in the dark, it just turned on its light, creating a comfortable place for itself to stand. It surrounded itself with exactly what it needed until daylight returned and gave off enough extra light to help all around it, too. I always felt a kinship with that lonely streetlight. Something about the way it was living felt true to me. It lived in hope.

Over the years, I've come to understand that in order to have light in my life, in order to have hope, I need to draw a circle for myself to stand in. Being surrounded by love illuminates just such a space, and although I can't completely control anything, I can create love in my life for myself, by loving God and by loving the people around me.

By generating my own love, my own light, my own hope—drawing a circle for myself and then reliably showing up to stand in it—I not only survive, but sometimes I'm able to throw off a little extra light into the darkness around me. And darkness is an important part of my story. I have felt it keenly in my life, but perhaps my acquaintance with the dark has made me sensitive to even the smallest hint of light. A light becomes more useful when the darkness around it increases.

When I was fourteen years old, I felt conflicted about my Mormonism—chafing against its constraints, even as I took comfort from the hope I found there. Tired of feeling pulled both ways, I picked up my Book of Mormon one night and decided to put Moroni's promise to the test. I tried to read with real intent over the next few weeks, and after I'd finished, I prayed hard.

And the increase of peace I received from those prayers came with a sense of place—like looking at a map with a bright dot that says, "You Are Here." It wasn't an undeniable witness of truth, but it was real and personal: a witness that I was standing in my place and need only turn on my light. I still refer to this as my "pesky" experience with the Book of Mormon, because I've never been able to extinguish its hope. I've never wanted to, no matter how much my head insists I should.

My connection to Mormonism has always felt more personal than doctrinal. We each need a certain quality of light to illuminate our darkness, and my darkness isn't born of big questions seeking big answers. Rather, it's a need to connect the small dots of my human experience, and then find a connection with others.

As I look back across my lifetime of membership, I see a long string of lights from which I continue to draw hope—people and ideas, feelings and experiences—a collective brightness of small things to which my heart returns when I need spiritual rest. They are uniquely mine, gifts that perhaps only I can see, but they illuminate my path and nudge me forward. There was so much to love in my Mormon upbringing.

I loved the Primary songs, that later became lullabies for my babies, "Tell Me the Stories of Jesus" and "Little Purple Pansies" and "Whenever I Hear the Song of a Bird." Laughing at the chorister who had saggy skin wagging from her aging arms, hair piled up miles high above her head and a tremulous voice that was louder than the room was big. But even then, knowing she had other things she could be doing and being grateful she was there, I took comfort in her kind hand, moving up and down with each note to show us where to sing. I wanted to grow up to wear the same white patent leather boots.

I loved the organ, booming its familiar hymns, while my mother beat time for the congregation, her white baton swinging with feeling and her lipsticked mouth worshipping in a deep red alto O. She led the music as if God himself had called her to it. Because he obviously had.

I loved the kids I grew up with, the same faces year after year, their dresses, their curled hair, their questions, their freckles, their boredom, their rebellion, their snickering, the inside jokes, the walks home after.

I loved my teachers, all the unlikely ones who showed up anyway when we did nothing to earn their time or love. We listened with one ear, watched with one eye, kicked the chair in front of us with both feet and ran our mouths nonstop in an attempt to prove that we already knew much more than anyone could teach us. Still, I remember treats in a battered aluminum pan. A handbag on the table, next to an open lesson manual underlined in careful pencil. Glimpses of my faith through a different mirror than the one I lived with. A flannel board, a magnet for the fridge, a token to remind me that my teacher cared, but Jesus cared about me most of all.

I loved the dresses my grandma made, years of Sunday ruffles in patterns and fabrics picked just for me. No one ever had the same clothes I had. How could they? Sitting next to her in church one day, I heard her sing that God is love and realized, with satisfaction, I already knew that—somehow she and God had made it plain.

I loved the fabric of our ward. Families lined up in their Sunday best, throwing off their daily lives and showing up like clockwork. Kind bishops, crying babies, missionaries who caught a hail-Mary haircut and were off to save the world—or perhaps themselves. Mothers who never doubted. Grownups knowing who I was and where I came from, caring where I went next. The booming man in the seersucker suit, the barrel-chested janitor, the head cheerleader, the orthodontist who loved poetry, that woman always on the second row, stick-straight in a fox fur, its pointy face pinned just below hers. The same characters in every performance, pillars of my childhood faith. There was a hint of eternity in the constancy of it, so much humanity in the details.

I loved youth leaders, their hours so freely spent—the man who taught me waterskiing, his zinc-white nose a legend under his threadbare hat, circling the boat as I dropped the rope again and again and again. He ignored my begging, my chattering teeth, promising if I'd try just once more I'd see. He knew I could even as I insisted I couldn't. He was right.

I loved suddenly being old enough to sing in our ward choir, everyone showing up at 6:00 a.m. Friday mornings to spend an hour lost in the wonder of God so loving the world. Easter cantatas and Christmas miracles, "The Battle Hymn of the Republic" in July and tears on the cheeks of the conductor when we raised the last amen. And it was good.

I loved the complexity. Things I didn't understand, things that spoke to my heart directly. Doctrines that answered one question but raised a dozen more. The secret feeling I was smarter than the teacher. The realization I knew nothing at all. Holy envy of another's truth. The beautiful language of the scriptures, fantastic stories in equal parts faith-promoting and troubling. Ideas much too big. Light through cracks. People called good who I knew did bad things, and people called bad who I knew to be good. Prayers answered or ignored. Figuring out which rules mattered and which never would. The tree of polygamy that offended deeply, but produced good fruit like me. Learning to keep walking while my heart and brain wrestled it all.

I loved summer reunions, ancient cousins swapping genealogy in the dappled shade of a small-town city park, picnic tables heaped with Jell-O and funeral potatoes and six kinds of cake, the buzz of children and swatting of flies, and everyone eager for the blessing on the food. I loved the blessing itself, its familiar cadence, its second nature phrases, the thankful language of food and family, the sustenance of belonging.

The moments of light that began in my childhood have continued as I've lived my Mormon life, in and out of wards, in and out of callings, in and out of belief, of faith, of hope. I gather them, I guard them. I am in the process of staying, the process of becoming myself. And I am a Mormon in ways so deep, I've never figured out how to reach or turn them off. If you're going to say I'm not a good Mormon, you may as well say I'm not a good me. Because I'm not sure how to be anything but this.

For me, being a Mormon isn't a destination, it's a path—a way to something better, a process of hope. And hope is what carries me from one moment of darkness and uncertainty to my next. I'm not sure why Mormonism has always given me the kind of hope I need in order to draw my circle of light, because it gives me plenty of less desirable emotions too. But not being able to explain it doesn't make it less real, valuable, or useful. Hope is both where and how I live.

Every time I act in accordance with my hope, I am shown a glimpse of my own light. Surely that's the point of church: to allow us to catch sight now and then of what is possible. Whether it is something about

Mormonism or something about myself, I believe in the hope at the bottom of it all. It speaks peace to my lonely heart.

Why do I stay? Because I want to be a light much bigger and brighter than I am now, and I feel it could happen if I'm willing to keep showing up with the wounded and weary and disenfranchised every Sunday, each of us a little less alone when we recognize something true in the other, standing together in a circle of collective light we draw for ourselves and anyone who needs it.

As a child, I learned of loneliness, and was called to turn on my light. I've been learning to use that light ever since. To be a Mormon is to be in a process—of conversion, of doubt, of faith, of hope, of wending our infinite separate ways. We're always engaged in finding our path, or staying on it. We're always in the process of becoming who we can be. So I stand where I am and draw my circle. I am here.

Lessons from My Grandma's House

Kimberly Applewhite Teitter

My grandma Melba was the greatest woman in the world. My mom was great too, but she didn't spoil me like Grandma did. Melba was a superstar. She taught for over forty years in Greene County, North Carolina, where nearly everybody knew her. She was always classy, never rowdy, and wherever she went, people were always chasing her down to say "Hello," give a "Thank you" for a service she had provided, or just to share a laugh. She was active in the community and held the respect of everyone from the humblest farmer to the local bourgeoisie. As important as she was in the eyes of others, in *her* eyes, her grandchildren were the only ones (besides the Lord) who were worthy to be praised. My father was her only child, so she could devote a lot of energy into being our biggest fan in the twilight of her life. Whenever I performed a musical number, crossed an academic threshold, or achieved some honor, she always made a proud yet heartfelt scene, often standing up and dancing in celebration.

Our usual Sunday routine involved arriving three minutes late for church but being right on time for the Sunday repast at Grandma Melba's house afterward. We'd stay through the evening, gorging ourselves on fried chicken and cabbage and finishing off with Edwards brand strawberry cheesecake and Lorna Doone cookies while surfing channels on her satellite TV. We rarely talked about why it was that we didn't spend the morning at church together, like many extended families we knew; we were mostly just grateful that the hour and a half she spent at her African Methodist Episcopal Zion church gave her enough time to get back home and prepare the meal while we slogged through our three-hour Mormon Church block.

The Church of Jesus Christ of Latter-day Saints has been the only faith home I have ever known. The story goes that my mom first spoke to the elders on the deck outside our house because my father wasn't home at the time they were out tracting, but she invited them back to teach our family. My mom and my oldest brother were the first to get baptized in 1990, when I was two years old and my older brother was four; my dad held out for *several* more sets of missionaries until finally taking the plunge two years later. As far as I know, Grandma Melba never criticized my dad's decision to join the church; I don't even remember her talking about how odd it was that besides us there were *no* Black families at our church.

I do remember that Grandma Melba's house was the place where I learned the most about what it meant to be Black. I can still remember her kindhearted laugh, followed by her sharp correction, when I asked if she was white because she had lighter skin than I did. She taught me about the Civil Rights contemporaries of her day, and at her house we watched many Black historical movies that kids our age probably had little business watching. Grandma also demonstrated the expansiveness of the Black family. Her house was the anchor of the family farm, where her younger brother lived and her youngest sister came as faithfully every Sunday as we did. She and my other grandmother were great friends, and she even hosted my mother's siblings for occasional dinners. Her love extended to our church family, even though she wasn't a member. She often joined us in the pews and politely greeted our teachers and friends. She was a faithful woman, doing what it took to keep our family together.

The hours we spent at my grandmother's house are countless, but as I reflect on the question of why I stay, two instances keep replaying in my mind. The first is from my junior year of high school. My brother and I were home for Christmas, he from college and I from the residential magnet school I had just begun attending. I sat in the coveted leather rocking chair, marveling that we could watch the Mormon Tabernacle Choir Christmas special on BYU-TV on my grandma's satellite network all the way in North Carolina. My family was gathered around watching the choir's Christmas special. They were singing

"Betelehemu," and we were wondering why Alex Boyé (whose face we always eagerly sought out in the sea of white faces) didn't sing the solo in that *Nigerian* song. As the camera panned back over the choir, all of a sudden I found my eyes glued to the screen, thinking I was witnessing an earthquake in Salt Lake City. I gasped and then realized that it was *not,* in fact, an earthquake, but rather the usually stoic choir subtly swaying to the African beat. I doubled over laughing, amused at the awkwardness of the choir's attempted cultural crossover. Out of the corner of my eye, I saw my grandmother also seemingly shaking with laughter only to realize quickly, as my father rushed over to her, that she was having a seizure, related to an illness (pancreatic cancer) found two months earlier in that beautiful dancing body, an illness I had only recently learned about and barely understood. At that time, Grandma had enough up days with her downs that I thought she would come through, just as she had everything else in her life. In some ways, we were lucky to be away during those times, because we didn't see how much she suffered, but it made her death a couple of months after that Christmas even more shocking.

The other important memory at my grandma's house was from two or three years earlier, when I was still in middle school. My dad was in the rocking chair this time, while my grandma and I sat on her red-patterned sofa. Two missionaries from our church were sitting across from us on a matching loveseat. They had been coming over to grandma's house for a few weeks now, and I was thrilled at the prospect of having her join us regularly in the pew where my immediate family had been sitting for the past ten years. Other family members had taken the discussions before, but they had all been too Baptist to trade in their shiny halos for green horns, as the Southern convention went. But I was *sure* that my grandmother was going to make it to the water and be baptized.

I don't remember much of the discussion that took place that day, but I do recall Grandma asking my dad some very pointed questions about a certain doctrine that differed from what she believed, and Dad was doing his best to respond. I've never asked him about the moment that came next, maybe because it was too painful for both of us. Perhaps he had been anticipating her question and had feared it would come to this moment, because when she asked it, he blurted out the answer to get it over with. At any rate, as the conversation ensued, my ears perked up to this gem of a non sequitur: "Well," my dad said matter-of-factly, "there was a time when Blacks couldn't hold the priesthood."

From that moment on, everything around me moved in slow motion while thoughts pulsed through my head at the speed of light. I remember looking down at my own brown-skinned arms, then past them to the blood-red carpet underneath, then up ahead at the curio stand in the corner that held my grandma's treasures: a "best teacher" award, her large-print Holy Bible and triple combination, and pictures of my brother and me. The wicker basket columns holding up the glass shelves blended in with the wooden bars that formed a trellis separating the den from the kitchen. In that moment those bars formed my mind's prison, blocking the synapses that were attempting to fire from my brain to my feet to get me to *run* and be anywhere other than in my skin, in that room, at that moment.

The last thing I dared to look at was my dear grandmother, the greatest woman in the world, shaking her head furiously and decisively with her eyes closed.

"I won't, Ricky," she told my father. "I won't hear anymore."

I started to come back from this astral projection to my own personal hell, my mind most clearly grabbing hold of one thought to ground me.

Why did he tell her? Why did he tell her that now?

It's interesting to reflect on that being my first conscious response back then. As I write this in 2020, the world feels as though it's on fire. My husband, our two little girls, and I have been in our spacious but seemingly ever-shrinking apartment in Salt Lake City for the better part of three months, trying to keep ourselves from contracting a virus that appears to be most severely impacting the heavily melanated among us. My heart is in a constant prayer for my angel parents who live 2,000 miles away and are continuing their work as healthcare providers to vulnerable populations. Within the last few weeks, just as people have been getting anxious for their lives to get back to normal, the news of Ahmaud Arbery came to light—a young man, Black like me, killed by two white vigilantes while out jogging. Since then, the names of other Black individuals taken from us before their time have risen to the top of an ever-increasing list written on my soul. *Breonna*

Taylor. George Floyd. Rayshard Brooks. The names swirl around me, as I think about being trapped in that room with my grandma who was also taken before her time—in part, by the same social determinants of health that make the current virus more fatal to Black and Brown communities. And the one aspect of the scene that I can't remember—as clearly as the squeak of the leather chair my father awkwardly shifted in, or the laser beam light reflecting off the curio shelves from the lamp framing my grandmother's face, or the darkness in the kitchen behind it which matched the darkness of my despair in that moment—is the missionaries who were sitting right across from me. I can't remember them because they were silent, as silent back then as the church I love has been to condemn the racism of today.

When I reflect on these things, I feel a bit of shame at my teenage naïveté, to think that my first reaction was to be angry at my father instead of more reactionary to the system we were both caught in. I wish I could blame it on being a kid, but by that age I was pretty savvy as to how the world worked. Though I had never heard the term *intersectionality*—the theory that the intersection of one's social identities (class, gender, race, sexuality, etc.) contributes to oppression and discrimination—I had already put together that to be young and smart was one thing; to be "young, gifted, and Black," as my dad once quoted to me from the old Nina Simone song, was quite another entirely; to be a young smart Black *girl* added different complexities; and to be a young smart Black *Mormon girl in the South* provided enough challenges to make my head spin.

Still, I had always felt up to the challenge, especially when it came to defending my faith. I played the part of Molly Mormon as best as I could, memorizing scriptures, filling my quote box with lines from obscure general authorities who were gone long before my time, learning to play deep-cut EFY tracks on the piano, and watching *On the Way Home* and *The Touch of the Master's Hand* so often that the tape on the VHS wore thin. I did what I was taught and then some, feasting on the words of Christ, trying to stave off that gnawing feeling of being out of place, desperately nurturing the belief that the gospel works for everyone. Up until that day with grandma and the missionaries, I thought my family was the only Black family in the pews because of good old fashioned Southern racism, not because of the church's own history with racial issues. Even if I didn't feel like I belonged to the church, the church belonged to me, and that was more than enough reason to love it as unconditionally as I did.

Other than the pain of my grandmother's refusal to join the church, I didn't think much about what had happened that Sunday afternoon, at least, not consciously, and tried to live my life in denial of what I had learned at her house that night. As I look back now though, I realize that this event may have laid the foundation for much of how I think about my membership in the church today, toward the development of guiding principles that have shaped my spirituality up to the present.

I can remember being in my high school library around the time my grandma was taking the missionary discussions (the library probably just as much a sacred space for me as church was at the time), browsing my favorite teen magazine, when I came across an article about a special school in New York City named after a man named Harvey Milk; it described the school as a place open only to kids who identified as gay, bisexual, or transgender, so they could go to school without being harassed or harmed.

Growing up fairly deep in the Bible Belt, I had never dreamed of going to New York City, had never heard of Harvey Milk, and "didn't know" any gay people, but as my big little heart pored over the pages, something deep within me was touched by the idea of a place where people who were different from others could go to be safe and I felt a desire to go there one day. Whether it was to visit, volunteer, or work, I wanted to do anything that would help those kids know that they deserved to feel safe—and deserved to belong. While I didn't have the chance to fulfill that dream (though it's still on my bucket list!), it was the beginning of my conscious desire both to commune with people who have been pushed to the margins of society and to empower marginalized people to carve out their identities and create their narratives, both flowing with and coursing against the dominant culture. Much of my current work as a psychologist and an advocate began to take shape in that small library.

Another pivotal moment from this time happened when one of my high school drama teachers announced that she was organizing a school choir to sing Black gospel music. The only exposure I had to gospel music at that point was whatever played on the radio during the eight-minute ride to church, or on the rare occasions that we would visit the Baptist church where my mother grew up. I can remember being a little girl bracing myself against the hard wooden pews and trying to hide my head so that the cacophony around me would lessen. My favorite Primary song at that point was "Reverence Is Love," so it was *especially* hard for me to understand why these people were doing so much rocking and clapping to the music *in church*. I'd look over at my mom and be somewhat disoriented when I saw her singing something other than what came from "the green book" I was used to at my church; but I also remember noticing, even *as* a child, how much *like* a child she looked when she was singing those songs, almost as though she was in her safe place. So when the school gospel choir started up, I joined immediately.

The best way to explain how significant that particular decision was is to fast forward almost fifteen years. It is 2018 and I'm sitting in the most unlikely of places, part of a 350-person choir at ten o'clock in the evening, with the iconic bright golden organ pipes of the church's Conference Center behind me as I'm watching the "Empress of Soul," Gladys Knight, pace back and forth nervously on the stage beneath me. She is surrounded by musicians and numerous amplification devices and monitors to help send the sound back to the choir. We are preparing for the "Be One" celebration, the 40th anniversary commemorating the lifting of the priesthood and temple ban for Black people, but in that moment, we were running into the problem of producing a gospel sound in a building that wasn't made for that type of music. The musicians waited patiently as the sound engineer adjusted the knobs then tested their individual instruments as he instructed. In the moments of stillness, the musicians began to improvise on their instruments, eventually morphing into a song I had heard years ago:

> *Jesus, be a fence all around me everyday.*
> *Jesus, I want you to protect me as I travel along the way.*

I mouthed the words softly and let my eyes droop, almost as my mother did in the pews of Beautiful Valley Free Will Baptist Church. I was contentedly resting in this daydream when a white woman next to me asked, "Do y'all sing this song in your choir?" Yes, the Be One choir was intended to be a symbol of unity, but was in fact a

Transformer-esque mash-up of different choirs and singers from across the country, including the Debra Bonner Unity Gospel Choir (which I was a part of), the predominantly Polynesian Divine Heritage Choir, and Gladys's own Saints Unified Voices. The singer addressing me was in the (already colloquially branded) "Tab Choir," and was not familiar with the song, but she apparently noticed that several other voices around us had joined in with me.

"No. It's just one I know."

"Where did you learn it?"

I paused for a moment before responding, "I'm not sure exactly, but as Black people in the church, you have to pick this stuff up from somewhere, or else you don't have anything to talk to other Black people about." And so it was.

When I joined that little gospel choir in high school, oh, how the kids stared! It was probably the Blackest thing I had participated in to that point, and I felt like all the *real* Black kids there knew it. It wasn't that I wasn't Black, but I had little cultural capital in the Black community for various reasons, being Mormon the biggest of them all. There were many Black churches in our town, and the Church of Jesus Christ of Latter-day Saints *wasn't* one of them. I didn't know the songs the other kids knew; I wasn't used to moving as the other kids moved; and when I felt the spirit, I didn't sway and bounce and run with my head to the sky like the other kids did. I was acutely aware of being a stranger in my own land. But when I heard gospel music, when I joined my voices with my peers, I felt the kinship of the ancestors join us all, in a way that was so intoxicating to me that I couldn't give it up. I learned from participating in that group how to have the courage to bring other experiences in to feed my soul as the spirit dictated to me, and that this spirit does not belong to one religious denomination. I felt that I had found something that I didn't know I had lost.

I wish I could say that I found a secret reservoir of the balm of Gilead "to make the wounded whole" or that I had a heavenly visitation to soothe my anguish, and that those were the things that helped me find the strength to keep the faith through the years. However, our Mormon stories tell us, perhaps better than most traditions, that even angels can't shield you from the pain and consequences of life. There have been many painful years I've spent fruitlessly engaged in the action of apologetics and ecumenicalism, seemingly to no avail, with my Southern Christian cousins; many years defending my career aspirations to my white in-laws and busybody ward members, even as it sometimes caused strain in my own marriage to dream differently than the typical Mormon girl; many years following the desires of my heart to be an ally to my LGBTQ siblings, while dodging the leadership roulette that makes same-sex advocacy okay one day and verboten the next.

Even within the safe spaces of the gospel, I sometimes struggle to feel comfortable, because my skin often doesn't have that "Mormon glow" of whiteness that people, at least in this country, have come to associate with the church. As I write this, I'm listening to my husband explain the nuances of systemic racism to an old friend, and my tired bones thank him. He is a bishop right now, and recently sent an email to the ward about the need for people with white privilege (as he holds) to reflect inwardly and repent of the sin of racism. As "woke" as he can be, and as nice as it is to borrow his privilege on occasion, it doesn't change that our relationship is a consequence of the radical acceptance during my teenage years that I would likely have to marry a white man in order to raise children in the church. I assume that my fellow members must recognize this on some unconscious level, but it has never stopped anyone from either leaning in too insensitively (asking, "How did you find the gospel?" while not asking my husband the same question) or ignoring the complexity all together (saying, "Give me your maiden name, so I can look up where your ancestors came from!" not realizing they are actually looking up the family history of my ancestors' oppressors). It also doesn't change the level of intimacy that I reserve for issues of race that my husband doesn't always have the experiences to empathize with or the skills to respond without intellectualization or defense.

Also troublesome for me was the conflict of my soul over the "policy of exclusion" of 2015, when I saw many white cisgender LGBTQ allies leave the church, exclaiming that this was the worst thing the organization had ever done. Had their proximity to privilege made them blind to the embedding, blooming, and weaving of racism into church culture, even with the shared experiences of marginalization? As the Black pioneer Jane Manning James said, "Is there no blessing for me?" Is there no room for me in their conceptualization of justice?

In other words, at the end of the day I'm *still Black*—I still have felt the weight of proving that I represent the church I've fought so hard for my entire life.

After weeks of pondering the question of why I stay, an adage I use frequently in my profession with therapy clients comes to mind: It's rarely effective to ask yourself "why," because you're usually looking for reasons to be hard on yourself or wish you did something different. I suppose when I look at it, the events of my journey thus far in the Church of Jesus Christ of Latter-day Saints are full of the kind of scenarios that would leave (and have left) many people bolting for the door. There's an improbability to the *whys* we tell ourselves, so that our stories of resistance and resilience grow even taller. A large part of my story of staying hinges on reframing those improbabilities into inevitabilities of discipleship.

I once remarked to a dear friend in the gay/Latter-day Saint intersection that even though he had moved on to other faith communities, everything he did seemed to be distinctively Mormon, from the way he talked to the way he set his passions. He responded with one of the wisest phrases I've heard: "Mormonism is my native tongue of faith. To really communicate what I mean in that very delicate intersection of intellect and spirit, of course I'm going to express it in my native language." I realized that this same spirit had guided me through many of the trying times of my life, maintaining the comfort through the discomfort and giving me a place to belong.

Two years ago, during that first rehearsal for the Be One Celebration Choir, Sister Knight stood before a room of people who have now become some of my closest friends and associates, a room full of all the colors of the skin-color rainbow. She boldly said, "God chose this choir, and God chose you to be in this choir." In that moment, all I could do was to remember, remember, as my soul looked back and wondered.

I remembered that one night in 1999 when my family and I stayed up late and went to the meetinghouse, where someone had set up a small TV for us to watch a broadcast of Gladys Knight speaking at Women's Conference after she joined the church. I remembered that moment in the middle school library many years ago, where I opened my heart to seeing the humanity of the LGBTQ community I didn't know I had met or would meet. I remembered that old high school gospel choir, and how the love of the music of my people grew through those experiences with people with whom I did not share a church home. I remembered the hours I spent in front of a mirror, smoothing down my hair and doing my make-up, before going to church dances where no one wanted to dance with me. I remembered dreading navigating with every romantic partner how they were going to tell their parents they were dating a Black girl. I remembered wondering if I wasn't just wasting my time worrying about it, since Harold B. Lee said not to marry outside your race anyway.

I remembered how, years after, when I thought the struggles of my heart had resolved when I met my eternal companion and had our first beautiful child, my husband brought me to Utah kicking and screaming, as I turned to look at the East Coast as Lot's wife looked back toward Sodom. I remembered the sleepless nights of that previous year, wondering if I wanted the exhaustion of a marriage where I would forever have to encrypt my experiences with the cipher of racism and patriarchy, strewn between that and my own need to move away from the ways my spirit recognized more readily when back in Sodom. I remembered the first three miserable months after moving to Utah, doing my own projects in my apartment that faced the noisy and very active Union Pacific trains, and trying to maintain some semblance of self-esteem while waiting for a job or a friend. I looked back and wondered that the first space I embraced after moving here, the Genesis Group, only came to my mind because of a dear friend, a white gay man whom I had met through my association with Affirmation. I looked back and wondered as I remembered walking through the door of that first Genesis meeting and hearing the song that I had learned with that high school choir many years before: "*Oh Lord, how excellent is thy name. There is none like you, Jesus. Excellent is thy name. In all the earth, Jesus, excellent is thy name.*" I looked back and wondered, remembering how hard it was to go up to the choir director, now my dear mentor and second mother, and sing the song my heart wanted to sing through the sorrow while I auditioned for that choir. I thought about how hard it was to balance the rough patches of navigating a new group with the reality that if I didn't go there, I wouldn't have *anywhere* else to go. I looked back and wondered how I made it through those conversations with my mom when she'd look at my pain and ask,

"Why don't you leave [the choir]?" I wondered how I made it through the conversations with myself during those sleepless nights, when I'd ask, "Why don't you leave [this relationship]?" I wondered how I made it through conversations with dear friends and professional mentors, where they'd look at my lack of productivity and ask, "Why don't you leave [Utah]?" I wondered how I made it through the countless conversations with friends, acquaintances, associates, that random representative from that random Christian fellowship I tried to befriend, and anyone else who felt their opinion was worth weight, when they would ask, "Why don't you leave [the church]?"

I wondered what my grandmother would say, or better yet how she would *dance*—if she were alive—seeing me stay in this church, in this marriage, in this state, in that choir, long enough to receive the invitation for our group to sing with Gladys Knight. I wondered at the things I had learned that gave me the faith and the evidence to know that death brought her dancing feet back to life.

It's fitting that today, as the coronavirus pandemic threatens its second wave and as the fight to end racism rages on, I find myself in the refuge of the living room of my childhood home in North Carolina, sitting on that red-patterned sofa that once belonged to my grandmother. I watch my ten-month-old baby cruise around near the spot where Grandma used to sit and watch her satellite TV; she has the middle name of *Jane*, after my mother's mom, but her quiet yet determined self-assuredness reminds me so much of Melba. I can already imagine her wrinkling up her face twenty years from now, telling someone that *no*, she isn't white just because she has lighter skin.

The living room is our sacred space for making music and holding our church-at-home, and it is here that I take my place on the other side of the sofa and listen for my grandma to speak to me. Since her death, I like to draw upon her wisdom, guidance, and faith. If Jesus is my mediator in prayer, my grandma is like my hype girl and ghost writer—I draw on her spirit when I need to be reminded of my worth, and when I want to know how to better align my will with the Lord's.

I suppose that to answer the question of why I stay, I could have succinctly said this: As I have stayed with God, God has stayed with me, and staying in the church has allowed me to see him stay in the spiritual language I know best. As someone with the experience of moving physical residences earlier than I desired, staying in one place seems to be the best way to know that you have everything you need, that everything that is sent to you will get there, and that everything you lost will eventually be found. If I had not stayed, I would not be able to see where God has brought me, from that day at my grandma's to the present. I would not be able to see how God has never left me, even when I felt at times that everyone and every other group had. Only he could have brought me from the "valley of sorrow" I have felt as I move through the effects of racism—which truly feels like the "enemy of my soul"—to the "exceedingly high mountains." From those heights, when the veil between heaven and earth is thinnest, my grandmother's presence is there to show me how my steps have been ordered by him. The experiences I've had have molded my heart and made it more perfect to serve him. Staying in my spiritual place has brought me blessings beyond measure, as well as the wisdom to trust the One who knows my end from my beginning.

I look forward to the day when I return to my heavenly home, which I hope looks something like the sprawling fields of our family farm in Greene County where my grandma's house still stands. I hope I can walk into judgment with the strength of my female ancestors behind me. In the "land where joy shall never end," I'll lay my burden down at the feet of my Savior, settle down with the greatest woman in the world, and finally be at rest.

I Began to Feel Blessed

Eric Samuelsen

I am a Mormon because I was raised in a Mormon family. I grew up going to church every Sunday, attending Primary and MIA. When I turned nineteen, I went on a mission to Norway. Why have I stayed? Because it has never occurred to me to leave.

Had I not grown up LDS, it is unlikely that I would have found the church on my own. But I don't regret my lifelong membership and activity. Which is not to say that I haven't been tempted, that I haven't suffered moments of doubt, difficulty, and heartsickness over retrograde policies and cultural cluelessness. Those of us who stay generally do so for legitimate reasons. Those who leave generally also have legitimate reasons.

It was on my mission when I first experienced cognitive dissonance in relation to the church. It wasn't just the authoritarian style of my mission leadership. Being somewhat naive, I thought mission rules were supposed to be harsh and arbitrary. And while the policy of racially determined priesthood and temple exclusion nagged at my conscience, it just didn't come up very often. After all, I was serving in blonde-haired, blue-eyed Norway.

No, that first ripple in my testimony came as the result of a talk by an LDS Church general authority at a mission conference. He declared confidently the reasons why we weren't baptizing and told us what we should do about it. Why were Norwegians not responding to our message? Pride, the sinful pride of you missionaries, he said, and disobedience. ("Balderdash," said the little voice in my head.) He left us with more unnecessary and arbitrary rules to follow—blue-suits-only was one, forcing me to leave my perfectly serviceable brown suit in the closet—and he mandated a new door approach that he promised would lead to much more mission success, as defined by more baptisms. The door approach was woefully ill-suited for the Norwegian culture and, frankly, kind of Gestapo-enough so that I thought it was likely to get us arrested. I did try it for most of one day—I was a district leader and felt I had to lead by example—until my companion begged me to stop. And we did nearly get arrested. And I had to face a dismaying reality—a general authority had spoken, presumably by inspiration, misidentifying the difficulties we faced as a mission and prescribing preposterous solutions. This was not supposed to happen.

Nor were his solutions instructively absurd, the blue suits a blood-on-the-lintels act of devotion. As time went on, in fact, I couldn't help but notice that the missionaries who had the most baptisms were those most dismissive of this particular general authority's prescriptions. Strict obedience was, quite specifically, what didn't work. And that gradual realization became increasingly devastating to me.

That general authority will remain nameless. For many years, I couldn't listen to him speak in general conference. Of course, he wasn't the only one whose talks I thought were best avoided. The wife of a former stake president once told me, "If you aren't filled with the desire to throw your shoe at the TV during general conference, at least occasionally, you probably aren't paying attention!" I came to realize that for leaders as well as for the rest of us, inspiration is at best intermittent.

Getting revelation is exceptionally difficult. When I'm struggling for an answer to a prayer, I can literally spend hours pondering, praying, and trying to listen. And I'm rarely certain that my prayers have been answered; often, subsequent events prove that I wasn't inspired at all. Culture is a powerful force, and its whisperings can drown out the still small voice, even if we can tell the difference between them.

The general authority in charge of our region was trying to come up with an answer to an intractable problem—the difficulty of preaching the Restoration to affluent western Europeans. Western American conservative culture tends to be authoritarian, and so he was led by his culture to an authoritarian answer. He was a cultural conservative and thought as one. It was wrong for me to have judged him or to have held onto my negative feelings for so long. He was a good man, struggling to hear and respond to the Spirit. It took me a long time to gain that more charitable perspective. Why did I seek that perspective? Because over the course of my missionary service in Norway, I gained a testimony. Yes, I was disillusioned. But I also began to feel blessed.

What does it mean to have a testimony? I want to use language with precision and specificity, and that means resisting culturally familiar, but imprecise usages and clichés. I do not ever say, for example, that "I know the church is true." Or, "I know that the Book of Mormon is true." I don't know what those words mean in those contexts. I don't know what "true" means in describing an organization of a sacred text. If I say "this book is true," I'm probably referring to Isaac Newton's *Principia*, not Second Nephi.

What I can say is this: Through service to others, total strangers, in fact, I began to have thoughts and feelings that seemed to me to have been externally generated. I would speak to someone in my halting Norwegian and suddenly be overcome with a rush of unanticipated eloquence. I would see a distant house late on a night wasted in fruitless tracting, and a thought would occur—don't go home, don't quit for the night. You need to get to that house now. And a door would open. Teaching a lesson, I would suddenly know that the doctrine we were teaching was irrelevant to this person's life and that I needed immediately to switch gears and talk about something else. And I would follow that impulse, and see a life transformed.

To what then can I testify? To something quite limited, it seems to me, but also at least potentially liberating. I can testify that I felt at times influenced by a power outside myself, and that I continue to feel so influenced. But it also works; pragmatically, it genuinely gets the job done.

When I got home from my mission in June of 1977, the first movie I saw was *Star Wars*; it was also the one I saw the next eight times I went to a movie. A few weeks later, when I got home from work, I saw that the new *Ensign* (July) had arrived. I leafed through it and read a talk by President Spencer W. Kimball, "A Gospel Vision of the Arts." This paragraph blew me away:

> For years, I have been waiting for someone to do justice ... to the story of the Restoration ... the struggles and frustrations; the apostasies and inner revolutions and counter-revolutions ... the transitions ... the persecution days.

I did not know at that point what I wanted to do with my life. But that article hit me like, well, like Luke Skywalker's missile hitting the Death Star. In an instant, sitting on the sofa in my parents' living room, I knew who I was and who I was supposed to become and what I was supposed to do. I would be a playwright, and perhaps at times an essayist and novelist, but mostly a playwright, and I would write, in part, about my own culture. Unsparingly, truthfully, compassionately, but with integrity, I would write about my people. Later, in college and in graduate school, I would find models for my own writing—Ibsen and Chekhov, Tom Stoppard and Athol Fugard, and Tony Kushner and his remarkable *Angels in America*. But that moment—reading that *Ensign* article—was what launched me. A revelation? A vision? Or just a flash of ambition? Whatever the source, wherever it came from, it began in a single moment and has lasted a lifetime.

The next moment of inspiration came in 1978. I was in a BYU choir, and we sang the world premiere of Robert Cundick's magnificent oratorio, *The Redeemer*. I was a tall bass and shared a riser with a tall blonde soprano. We chatted a bit during rehearsal breaks. At one point, she turned away, and I found myself looking at her, just the side of her lovely face, framed by her blonde hair.

It wasn't love at first sight, not at all. We were both in choir again the next fall and became friends. We liked a lot of the same books, we enjoyed the same music. Our relationship didn't turn romantic for many months. But at that moment, sharing a riser, singing a piece of music we both loved, I knew, absolutely *knew*, that this person was going to be an important part of my life. She was a girl I shared a riser with; it's entirely possible we would never have met again. But I knew in my heart that something beyond that choir and that music was happening. I didn't think, "That's the girl I'm going to marry." Turns out, it was, and our marriage has become the centerpiece of the last thirty-five years of my life. At the time though, all I knew was that something significant was going to happen in my life involving this person. Marriage and four children? I had no idea. Still, something spoke to me.

Of course, some will say that weird, impulsive feelings happen all the time without any religious meaning or context. People get inspired to pursue a career path, people meet and think, "Let's keep this conversation going." Others will say such feelings are just career "Eureka!"

moments or love-at-first-sight realizations, that invoking gifts of the Spirit is not required to explain common phenomena. And while that's perfectly true, nevertheless, I interpret these two experiences as meaning something special. I know that something to be a Mormon cultural construct—the Spirit revealed my career path and the personal importance of the woman I would marry. That's how I understand those experiences.

What this means for me is acknowledging God's hand in my life. In Doctrine and Covenants 59:21, we're told that "in nothing does man offend God" more than when we "confess not his hand in all things." That suggests to me that we're not just justified but maybe sort of obligated to say, "This was God speaking, this was inspiration, this was revealed." And that is what I believe.

Annette and I married, we had four children, and I began teaching at Brigham Young University. We had some joyful years, teaching theater history and theory and playwriting, writing and directing and researching. And experiencing genuine moments of spiritual growth and transcendence, as well as moments of cognitive, cultural, and spiritual dissonance.

Is it just me, or did everything get weird in 2008? That's my impression, at least. Before that, I'd write plays and they'd be well received and vigorously supported by the BYU administration. And then that stopped being true. A new university president was called who "knew not Joseph." More significantly, a new American president was elected. It is entirely my subjective impression of course, but it seems to me that during that time conservatives went crazy.

I was too new at BYU and in Utah to understand or be much affected by the events of 1993, the brutal excommunications of the September Six. But my testimony has been buffeted by subsequent events, by further moments of cognitive dissonance. I think especially of my LGBTQ friends and family members who feel, with justification, that there's no legitimate place for them, that they will always be, at best, second-class citizens of the church. And it breaks my heart.

Some people leave the church because the pain of staying overpowers the desire to remain. Some of our brothers and sisters who leave do so because they need to avoid continuing pain. Perhaps a short answer to the question "Why do I stay?" is that I haven't been hurt enough to impel me to leave. The church has never hurt me. BYU is another matter entirely. While I loved my twenty years on the BYU faculty, loved my students and colleagues and classes and plays, my time there ended badly, and hurtfully. But at that point, I do believe that Heavenly Father saved me, mostly by making me really, really sick. Time for more forgiveness, time for humility, and perhaps a more nuanced understanding. Those events certainly never drove me to want to leave. I stay because I think there's good I can accomplish by staying.

There are times when we need to speak up, allow our voices to be heard. It is wrong, morally wrong, for BYU to expel good students who have, due to a crisis of conscience or faith, decided to leave the church. That policy is indefensible, and incompatible with basic gospel principles of agency and accountability. As I look back at the mission conference talk that so bothered me, it seems another example of practices borrowed from corporate culture overriding the personal, individual touch favored by the Savior. And while I applaud the online Gospel Topics essays on history and doctrine, the perspectives they offer are not reflected in lesson manuals and other approved materials.

I am fully aware that the organization to which I have given my lifelong allegiance is, in many ways, not all it should be. I know of its checkered history, especially on issues of race and LGBTQ rights. I know that it is only fitfully progressive. I think it unlikely that I would ever have become a Mormon if not raised in the faith. I probably would have become a Democrat, but I'd probably be leaning to vote for Jill Stein rather than Hillary Clinton.

Mormonism has become my home, just as the Democratic Party has. I don't believe in magical revolutionary solutions. I prefer to work within the organization, to do whatever good I can to nudge things forward bit by bit rather than hope for an improbable breakthrough. That's not to say that improbable breakthroughs can't happen, as we all learned in 1978. But in the meantime, I do what I can, function where I am.

Meanwhile, there are good reasons to stay. I have a friend, a former stake president, who told me a few years ago about his awesome church calling. Twice a week, doctors and nurses and other medical personnel provide free health care to anyone who needs it; his calling is to organize those events. All supplies are free of charge, including medications. I asked how many of the people who took advantage of this opportunity were undocumented immigrants. He said that his instructions were specific and clear—they weren't ever to ask. And they don't. He said they were also told that the press was discouraged from reporting on the program. This isn't a public relations project, he said, it is pure compassion, Christianity at its finest. And therefore the best calling he's had in a life of service.

So that's also why I stay. Ultimately, Eugene England was right—the church is as true as the gospel. And when we say "the church," what do we mean? I don't often think of the larger institutional church. I mean my ward, the 300–400 friends and neighbors with whom I so happily worship every Sunday of my life. It does indeed take a village to raise a child. Within Mormonism, it takes a ward. I am forever grateful to the Primary workers and Young Men's and Young Women's leaders and teachers who have served my family so faithfully, who have befriended and loved my children. I also think of my own opportunities to stretch my compassionate muscles and serve.

A month ago, I was very ill. I called my home teachers for a blessing. One is from Mexico and speaks very limited English. But something, the Spirit, spoke to me and said that that brother should seal the anointing and bless me, and that he should do so in the language he was comfortable with, Spanish. As he laid his hands on my head and pronounced a blessing, I only understood a few words of what he said. But I felt something beyond the words—an almost overpowering feeling of love and kindness, what I believe was a personal communication from my Heavenly Father. The message was that I was going to be okay. My life was in his hands. He loved me and knew how much longer He needed me here. In the meantime, I received the message to be of good cheer. My eyes filled with tears, and as I looked in the face of my good brother, I could see he'd felt the same thing I did. And I looked at my wife, my anchor and my joy, and I knew we were together for a reason, even if it's not always clear what that reason might be.

Love. Kindness. Service. Love.

That is why I stay.

Eric Roy Samuelsen died on September 20, 2019.

God Works with Prepared Minds

Camilla Miner Smith

I was born in Nevada but grew up in Utah, the Beehive State, which I still love even though I have lived away from it in large cities for over fifty years. I love Mormon folk, including Mormon food, arts, and crafts. My comfort food is funeral potatoes and my long-deceased mother's lime Jell-O salad made with cottage cheese, pineapple, and mayonnaise. Recently, I purchased a cake dish with a tall beehive cover. I have a similarly shaped honey jar. I love Mormon crafts: The quilt on our bed was made fifty years ago by the Manhattan Ward Relief Society. It is a "hearts and flowers" pattern, two squares of which I sewed and embroidered myself. I love looking at it, including its flaws, and I love the hands that made it. I miss those sisters who have now passed on.

But my appreciation of these folk ways is not why I stay. The reasons I love the church are more conceptual and intangible.

I grew up in a family that valued both science and religion. I believe the gospel of Jesus Christ embraces all truth. My grandfather, Edward Christian Eyring, told his son, my uncle, the scientist Henry Eyring, before he left on his mission, "Henry, in this church you don't have to believe anything that is not true. If it's not true, it's not part of the gospel." In my own experience, it is a waste of time to believe something that is not true, because you can't get anywhere on an untruth. You head in the wrong direction or come to the wrong conclusions. What kind of God would deal in untruths?

I take the leap of faith. I believe there is a god, although I see God as plural. The word *Elohim,* meaning gods, is found more than 2,500 times in the Hebrew Bible. I love Mormonism because its understanding of

God includes the feminine as well as the masculine. I believe that even though God is all-knowing, he/they are limited to working within the laws of nature. I remember discussing evolution with my Uncle Henry, and he said he was not so interested in what happened after the Big Bang. What he wanted to know was what happened *before* the Big Bang.

I think life has core truths and meaning, which I am striving to discover. I believe all knowledge and experience result in personal growth and lead us closer to the truth. I also feel an obligation to continually learn more, to challenge long-held beliefs in light of new understanding. I feel I can get closer to the core of Truth with the church as my teacher.

Trying to discern what is true is challenging because there are different kinds of truth. For some, truth is what can be scientifically and empirically provable. Others have a wider view. In the foreword to his *History of Western Philosophy,* the philosopher Bertrand Russell said the reason he studied philosophy was because he felt all the important questions were not answered by science. Russell posed such questions as: How should I live? What is justice? Why do I love one person and not another or find one thing beautiful and not another? He felt philosophy answered such questions. For me, philosophy is too academic a way to explore these ideas. I have found religion a more active and experiential way of addressing such questions. In a truly religious life, you contemplate, explore, and then act, and in this way come to a broader and deeper understanding. To be limited to the scientifically demonstrable leaves one, I believe, without answers to some of life's most important questions. I believe there is truth in science and truth beyond science, which might be thought of as psychological, emotional, and even spiritual truth.

For years I have been on a quest to understand what it means to be human. I am president of the LSB Leakey Foundation, which funds research into human origins, ape studies, behavior, and DNA. All humans have our origin in Africa. Mitochondrial Eve, our most recent common ancestor, the maternal ancestor of all living humans, has been traced to a verdant paleo oasis in the Kalahari Desert of Africa. The oldest DNA lineages are found in the San people of Southern Africa.

Seeking to understand how we differ from other primates, especially in our search for God, I once asked Jane Goodall if she had ever observed a kind of proto religion in chimpanzees, our closest living ape relatives and the primates with whom we share 98.8% of our DNA. She said she had seen behavior she considered akin to what we call awe or wonder. Normally, chimpanzees are afraid of water, but in Gombe, Tanzania, where she studied them, she found that chimps travel together to a waterfall. When chimpanzees are calm, their hair lies flat; when they are frightened, their hair stands straight up. When a group of them gather at the edge of a waterfall, their hair partially stands up as they watch the water cascade over the rocks. Goodall saw this behavior, which the chimpanzees seemed to seek, as akin to and evidence of the awe humans feel in contemplating God.

A way we differ from the other apes is in altruism, caring for those who are not part of our own family. Chimpanzees kill offspring that are not theirs. So do gorillas. But if what makes us human is altruism, I believe it makes perfect sense for us to worship Jesus Christ, the ultimate exemplar and embodiment of altruism. John 1:1 says that in the beginning was the Word. Christ is the Word of God. We should not underestimate the power of metaphor. As humans, our brains are uniquely built to use metaphors and symbols, of seeing one thing in relation to another. When we use words, we are using symbols to represent real things or thoughts. This is how we understand anything.

When I was in France a few summers ago, I visited the Gargas Cave in the Pyrenees. This early prehistoric cave has animal drawings and more than 200 handprints left by early humans more than 30,000 years ago. The low ceiling of the cave has thousands of lines left by human fingers in soft clay, now covered by calcite thousands of years old. One observes small animal bones pounded into the cracks in the cave walls. I asked our guide what he thought explained the animal bones in the cracks and he surmised it was like the Wailing Wall in Jerusalem—a way to send messages and connect with the power beyond the wall, to connect with something ineffable, perhaps something akin to Deity. This suggests that part of what it is to be human is to quest for understanding and to communicate with the mystery that lies beyond the wall. I believe there is a connection between the paintings I saw on the walls of prehistoric caves and what happens in churches, mosques, synagogues, and temples.

The caves of Cro-Magnon are extraordinary, with evidence that when we became fully modern humans, we went into the caves for ceremonies. There is no evidence of living in the caves, no food remnants, no fires. Lascaux in France and Altamira in Spain, which I have been fortunate enough to visit, are caves of great beauty and ritual meaning and seem to have been important ceremonial centers. In the caves there is evidence of music, art, and ritual. For example, paleoanthropologists have found small bone flutes and surmise that the acoustically vibrant caves probably housed both percussive and vocal music, which leave no trace. The cave walls also display magnificent art, mostly graphics of animals and handprints. All this suggests that we seem to have a deep need for spiritual meaning and ritual expression.

For me, that need is met in part by my membership in the Latter-day Saint religious community. In my church calling as a public relations and interfaith specialist, I am intimately involved in the larger interreligious community in the San Francisco Bay Area. In that capacity, I am involved in substantial interfaith work, including serving on the board of the Interfaith Center at the Presidio, where I work with clergy and members of other faiths. One of the exercises we use is called Appreciative Inquiry in which we tell one another what we love most about our faith. This is what I say: Latter-day Saints see this life as a schoolroom where we can learn to become more godly. We are encouraged to have direct communication with God; we stress the importance of families; and we are taught to understand, love, and serve others. For me, the church is like a schoolmaster, teaching us how to be caring, encouraging self-discipline, fostering a communal dialogue about how we should live, and taking responsibility for working out our own salvation through the atoning sacrifice of Christ.

I love to go to church, to sing the hymns, to learn new things from people who live very different lives from my own, and to share my experience and insights. In France, I went to church with the descendants of the cave painters (according to DNA studies, the Basques are descended from Cro-Magnon people) and was greeted with a kiss on both cheeks. We discussed, in French, the importance of loving our neighbors and what might be done to help others. I have friends who say they can do all that without going to church, but it has been my observation that many do not. If you don't have a community where you can discuss important issues and question your own behavior, you usually don't do it on your own.

I observe that if you try to be good, you usually are—especially if you are working together with others to do good. The collective experience is usually successful in helping a group to find the best plan or policy, especially when it includes humility, openness, a desire to listen, and a willingness to admit faults. Lately, I have been especially impressed with our church leaders giving sound counsel that prepared us for studying the gospel at home during this COVID-19 pandemic, how we have been asked to care for those less fortunate with food, and the practical help given during the financial crisis that has accompanied the pandemic.

I believe God can give me insight, direction, and wisdom I would not otherwise have. I have had answers to my prayers. I believe God speaks to us at times. I told a psychologist friend that I had heard voices in response to prayer. She responded, "Camilla, that is not good." After spending a few days doing research on our faith and learning that Latter-day Saints believe in communication from beyond the veil, she called back and said, "Camilla, it's okay." Her psychology reference books told her that if you come from a community that hears voices, you can hear voices and still be psychologically healthy.

When I was in graduate school in New York City, I had what I consider a crisis of faith. In a course on Black literature, I learned that the writer W. E. B. Du Bois was deeply attracted to the Bahai faith because he found most other faith traditions such as Christianity, Islam, and Judaism too tribal. Since that included my own very tribal religion, I decided I no longer needed to believe and no longer needed to follow all the rules of my faith. Initially, it seemed such a relief, like, as Fawn Brodie described it, "taking off a winter coat in the summer." But as I thought more about it, I realized tribes are just large families. A baby does not survive without a family. I concluded that belonging to a tribe makes the individuals within it strong because the circle of love and belonging foster healthy development. The problem with tribalism comes when we only look to the inside of the circle, facing inward rather than using the strength of that circle to face outward to the larger world where we can bless others. The Jews have a Hebrew term for this concept: *Tikkun olam,* repairing the world.

I value the Latter-day Saint concept of continuing revelation, a principle that allows for change as the church and society change. Such a change happened with President Spencer W. Kimball's reversal of the priesthood and temple restrictions for Blacks. I believe that decision was likely influenced by his long engagement with Native Americans in Arizona. He understood the need for inclusion. He was open to receiving revelation because of his background and experience. This is an example of my belief that God works with prepared minds. That is why it is so important for us to read the scriptures and keep our minds open to new ideas and new ways of looking at the world. I feel certain God would have wished us to have been prepared for that change earlier than it happened.

To conclude: I stay committed to the Church of Jesus Christ of Latter-day Saints and to what I consider Mormon Christianity because in so many ways I see God's hand at work there, including in my own life. The church helps me discover what is true and helps me act on those truths. I consider that kind of education is the primary purpose of this life.

The Lasting Pain of Thankfulness

Charles Shirō Inouye

I'm feeling unusually clear-headed these days, having recently finished a draft of a memoir that will probably be called something like "Zion Earth Zen Sky—Learning to Rake." It's a collection of haiku, along with memories of this and that.

I tried writing a short history because I haven't been very good about keeping a journal, and I wanted to leave something behind for my children—Mie, Leif, and Kan—and for their children. It's essentially a record of the moments when I most clearly felt the influence of the sacred in my life—the "small plates" of Charles, as it were, *à la* Brother Henry Eyring.[1]

I have to say it was a pretty helpful thing to do. For the first time, I think I've identified my leitmotif—the one thing I've had to work on most for the longest period of time.

Here are four things I learned by way of this family history.

One. I have often been surprised.

Two. My main weakness is a tendency to withdraw from situations and people I don't like.

Three. God's love has been a steady and constant influence.

Four. By obediently responding to the spirit, my weakness has been addressed in a way that has led to blessings and happiness for myself, and for many others.

Let me just say a few words about each of these points.

Life Is Surprising

I think I have a fairly good sense of why things are the way they are.

And, yet, when I wrote the memoir, I realized how often the events of my life were surprising and unexpected.

What does it mean when your life surprises you?

One possibility is that life is not boring. By way of a patient attending to the small things that define an LDS lifestyle—what I call raking—even routine things become meaningful, and the miraculous happens.

From this, I can only conclude that my "natural-man" (Mosiah 3:19) understanding of things is even more limited than I suspected, and that I've been blessed by staying in the game.

My Weakness

While still a graduate student, I had this experience. I was sitting with friends on the lawn in front of the Longfellow Chapel on Brattle Street in Cambridge, Massachusetts. It was a beautiful spring day in New England. The grass was green, the sky blue.

One of my friends said, "We don't learn anything in this church."

He was talking about how we cover the same ground over and over again.

"We're not really dedicated to living intelligently," I remember him saying.

Months later, we finished our graduate programs and went our separate ways. When I heard he and his family had left the church, I couldn't help wonder if it had something to do with his complaint about lack of learning.

True or false? We Latter-day Saints are actually not good at learning.

Let's say for the sake of argument that the answer is true. Perhaps the case can be made that, as a whole, we're not that intellectually curious. What the academy calls "liberal education," becoming free from prejudice by learning and study, is not a high priority for all Latter-day Saints. But does this mean that our default educational model—studying the same things over and over—is faulty?

I don't think so. There are many things to learn and different ways to learn them.

Take, for example, learning how to deal with your weaknesses.

My weakness is that I withdraw from others. Growing up in the isolation of the Utah countryside probably reinforced my natural inclination to shy away from things I don't like, which would include anything that I'm not used to. In the part of the world where I'm from, we say "it's different" when we don't like something.

From a gospel perspective, rejecting things that are different is a huge problem. We're supposed to be selfless. We're supposed to reach out to others. We're supposed to value and appreciate all of God's children.

So how does one go about learning how *not* to avoid people? How can I learn to be truly "in the world but not of it" (John 17:15-17)? Can I contribute to the building up of Zion, where we are of one mind and one heart, and there are no poor among us, if my range of experience and understanding lacks breadth and diversity (Moses 7:18)?

This is basically what my life story has been about—this struggle to turn a deeply rooted weakness into something like a strength. Over a very long period of time, I have gradually learned how to address my "original sin." But this happened only because I circled back to the same teachings over and over again.

The second line of Confucius's *Analects* reads, "Is it not a joy to have old friends come from afar?"[2]

There are different interpretations of this line. It's not perfectly clear who these "old friends" are. But many think they are the teachings we learn in our youth. As we grow older, they come back to us. And the reunion is joyous.

This is because only our "old" friends reveal to us who we really are. They do this by reminding us of who we once were. Their constancy gives us a way to understand how much we've changed—the ways we've learned a thing or two.

Now, about my specific weakness. My guess is that it's one that many other people share. It is the well-known problem of self-concern.

The Buddhist notion of *anatman* suggests that there is no such thing as the self. Having a clear and steady definition of who we are is often considered a good thing. But there is this alternative point of view that says it is delusional and harmful. To put it simply, our modern age of egocentrism flowed from a faulty epistemology that got in the way of enlightenment (even as it paved the way for The Enlightenment).

As man became the measure of all things, self-consciousness dethroned god and led many to nihilism. Its effects are still widely felt even now that the modern period is technically over and the postmodern possibilities of the post-human, neo-animistic, newly materialistic end of the secular period arise.

For anyone new to Buddhism, it might be shocking to hear someone say, "You don't exist!" But think of *anatman* in this way: Could you conceive of "you" without having some notion of "not-you"? If that's too hard to conceptualize, then think of apple and not-apple. Can we have a sense of what an apple is if we don't have a sense of what one isn't? These are lessons we learn from the Mahayana Buddhist thinker Nagarjuna.

If the answer is "not really" (which is what most would probably say), then this can only mean that "you" depends on something else. If this is true, if everything is contingent on something else, then what we call self-identity cannot stand alone as a clearly defined, unchanging, inherently stable essence.

In sum, the existence of anything and everything is conditional. Because of this "dependent arising"—one thing relying on another for its existence—nothing stands completely on its own.

If this seems like a silly trick of logic, try thinking about it this way: Think of all the things that are constantly influencing you. The food you eat. The air you breath. The people you meet. The images and sensations you take in. The thoughts you entertain.

It should be evident that we are constantly being influenced by things that are constantly changing us. Are you the person you were ten years ago? How about a day ago? Look at your hand. Is that the hand you had when you were a child?

Surely, we are forever learning and becoming something else.

Equally evident is our influence on all things. For this very reason, being too insistent about an unchanging self-definition of ourselves denies this truth about our deep connections with our surroundings. It gives us the impression that we stand at a distance, that our self, like René Descartes's *cogito*, is the ground zero of existence, the one thing we do know for sure.

Perhaps the best critique of *cogito ergo sum* (I think [critically], therefore, I am) is found in Nishitani Keiji's *Religion and Nothingness*.[3] In this book Nishitani argues that Descartes's doubt did not go far enough. At its worst, an insistent sense of self-identity prevents us from acknowledging, and therefore learning from, our connections with others. Modern Western epistemology makes us think we don't need the world, and that it doesn't need us.

But how could that possibly be true? The proposition certainly does not square with my experience as a member of the church.

As I said, my personal story is about an ongoing struggle with this delusional sense of self, with this notion that tempts me to keep a distance, to judge others, to over-value intellect, to not care about what others feel, to excuse myself from understanding the two noble Christian imperatives to love god and to love all of god's creations (Matt. 22:35–40).

So my life has been an extended attempt to stop falling prey to this tendency. I have needed to recognize my connections with everything, including with the gods and their many creations "of which I'm a part."

Given the already mentioned possibility of being surprised by life, and given the possibility of getting over my delusional notion of self, what actually saves me is what I call raking, this disciplined way of attending to the same practical tasks day after day, week after week, year after year.

My claim in "Zion Earth Zen Sky—Learning to Rake" is that "the genius of Zen is the genius of Mormonism. Both bring the abstract concepts of heaven down to earth. Both make the ordinary things of this world the way to salvation."

Our precise garden is made of imprecise sand. And so we have to get out there and rake and rake.

When the wind blows, we rake. When the rain falls, we rake.

Life is high maintenance. Getting by, day by day, takes a lot of work.

This can be frustrating. It can seem like a lack of progress. But this is how we learn about nothingness, which is not the same thing as "not learning anything." I believe my friend was wrong to criticize the way we cover the same ground over and over and over. But he was right to criticize our lack of learning. What we can learn from this constant raking is a simple yet salutary lesson: Doing something repeatedly can be the opposite of boring. In fact, it might be the best way to avoid ennui, anomie, alienation, nihilism, and so on. This way of loyalty and dedication makes everything in our lives a manifestation of god's love and goodness—even when we're making mistakes.

God's Love

A note to the reader. As you've noticed, I sometimes use the lower case when I write this word "god." I do this for the same reason that I've started to make the word plural. After all, there are many gods rather than only one. Right? Isn't that the idea that the temple teaches in such a poetic, trenchantly ironic way?

Why did you do it? Because she did it first.

Why did you do it? Because Satan tempted me.

Why did you do it? Because that's what happened in other worlds, everywhere.

God as a singular idea is beautiful, strong, and seductive. I am often drawn to concentrations of power. But god is a person, not an idea, and such a regard for power is often misleading. Who can deny that the idea of the one true God (or one true church) has killed millions?

By contrast, the gods are they whom we actually experience and know. For starters, there are *three* members of the godhead. They are one in intent and goodness. But they are also different from each other.

Add to this the Latter-day Saint (and Buddhist) notion of eternal progression, and you have a world of many gods.

The gods include us, at least potentially.

This polytheism is the Great Latter-day Saint Heresy. But it is also a reminder of an ancient Mahayana heresy. The idea that all sentient beings have Buddha nature, the ability to progress and to become saviors of the less fortunate, has been around for a very long time. As I tried to address in *The End of the World, Plan B,* whether we're considering Bodhisattvas or Saviors on Mount Zion, it's pretty much the same idea: We can become aware of our potential godliness and thus unleash ourselves from enslaving concepts like the self, separation, justice, nostalgia, and so on.[4]

This is the *Heart Sutra* speaking to us, where it says that "form is emptiness. Emptiness is form."[5]

We can learn. We can become perfected.

But this happens only if we embrace (and stay with) the lessons we first came to when we were children. As they say, practice makes perfect. A lot of "boring" relearning of the same lessons over and over is required to make us good at anything.

As I said, the process of writing a memoir made me realize how often and how powerfully the gods have made themselves felt in my life. For one thing, I would have died long ago without some help at crucial moments. Not only that, but I would not have learned how to escape from my prison of self-concern had I not been given the experiences that helped me see things differently, *even when* I was openly disregarding god's commandments.

Without a little divine intervention, I would not have been able to discover my deepest loyalties (since the process of understanding takes time). Unable to do that, I would have missed the point of my coming into this world. And that would have been a waste.

I don't know how much longer I'm going to live. But if I do live another day, I know I will try to spend it helping other people feel god's love.

That's why I'm here. That's why I'm writing this essay. I hope it persuades you to stay the course, to count your blessings.

I finally know my purpose because of things like Family Home Evening and ministering, and because of constant prayer and daily study. No one is so smart that they cannot learn from the simplest truths. This sort of raking has made the veil of forgetfulness thin enough to help us remember who we were in a previous existence, and what we and multitudes of others promised we would accomplish during this time we call mortality.

In short, I stay because I want to accomplish the goal of loving the world. Nothing else matters as much.

Being Blessed

Finally, the issue of being blessed. I learned a lot from my parents. I grew up on a farm with Dillon, Dwight, Warren, and Annie. We spent a lot of time together, and with our parents. It was not always pleasant. But we profited much from working hard.

I remember my father once spent a winter worrying about a rusty bolt. He stripped it while tightening it in the fall. He knew he had to get it out in the spring, somehow. Over the ensuing winter months, he thought about this problem, without doing anything about it.

When spring rolled around, the unavoidable moment came. We had no choice but to face up to the challenge of removing that bolt.

We sprayed on chemicals to dissolve the rust. We heated the bolt with an acetylene torch, so the expansion and contraction of the steel would free things up. We sacrificed an end-wrench by welding it to a long pipe. We refashioned it specifically for the purpose of getting that bolt out.

After all these preparations and after trying this and that, it finally came out.

When it did, my father exclaimed, "How could we be so lucky?"

I often reflect on that moment. Lucky? Is it luck when you've given something so much thought? Is it luck when you've bothered to make so many preparations? Is it luck when you've worked so hard to make something happen? What was my father thinking when he said we were lucky?

These questions arise because of a false assumption I have: that good things happen because we earn them. The atonement teaches us differently. We have a debt we can't pay. We succeed because of the grace that comes "after all we can do" (2 Ne. 25:23).

King Benjamin said it best. We could spend the rest of our lives helping other people, and we still would not be able to pay our debt to Jesus (Mosiah 2:21). None of us earns the salvation that his atonement makes possible.

This sentiment is expressed in the hymn "God Loved Us, So He Sent His Son."

> What debt of gratitude is mine.
> That in his offering I have part
> And hold a place within his heart.[6]

A Japanese way to understand this "debt of gratitude" is to say that we wear an *on* (or sense of obligation) because of Jesus's offering of his personal suffering and death. The idea is that when someone does something for you, you feel a need to pay them back in some way.

This nuance of debt is expressed in the Japanese words for "thank you," *Arigatō gozaimasu*. This is a humble form of the verb *arigatai desu*. The verb *aru* expresses possession and existence, as in *Hon ga aru*—I have a book, there are books. *Arigatai* is formed by a conjugation of the verb that expresses difficulty. *Aru* + *gatai* = *arigatai*. This means "hard to exist," or, by extension, "rare." For example, the expression *egatai tomo*—a friend that is hard to come by—uses this same conjugation: *eru* (to get) + *gatai* (difficult to) = *e-gatai*.

Jesus is a rare friend. His benevolence towards me is a singularly rare gift. I therefore feel this sense of *arigatai*. Receiving his blessings makes me feel a "debt of gratitude" that both lifts my burden of sin and also pains me because I realize just how precious the gift is. And it is, by the way, also a favor that requires me to reciprocate. It causes this some-times very painful awakening to my "debt of gratitude."

To put it simply, it has taken time (and practice) to feel thankful for what Jesus has done for me and for my family. Over time, the atonement has come to mean something very different. By taking the sacrament and remembering Jesus each Sabbath day, I have this "not-boring" reunion with my "old friend from afar," my *egatai tomo*. His unchanging love for me is the way I become aware of how much I have changed, whether for good or bad.

Why do I stay? I stay because, having felt god's love, I want to keep feeling it and to share it with others. I know what it has done for me, and I feel a debt of gratitude that makes things *harder* for me in some ways. *Arigatai*. I stay because, having learned the sorrowful feeling of thankfulness, I have faith that I can learn other important lessons.

I have made many mistakes, and I will continue making them. But I have also gotten over many of the burdens that have weighed me down. It is this wonderful process of learning that I wish more people knew about and trusted.

At the same time, I am fully aware of the ways in which both I and the institution of the Church of Jesus Christ of Latter-day Saints to which I belong are in need of reform and improvement. If anything, my life as a Latter-day Saint makes me increasingly sensitive to human failing and organizational weakness. My dealings with others are mul-tiplied by continued activity in the church, and this only increases my awareness of everyone's shortcomings and disappointments.[7]

That said, I must also say that most of my own problems with the institution of the church come from its modern (chauvinistic, com-petitive, prejudiced, materialistic, controlling, prideful) context, rather than from the ancient vision of possibility that the gospel provides. These problems present themselves to us precisely because we're gain-ing some clarity about what a true life might look like while living in a particular cultural context. Institutions can, and should, repent and do better, just as individuals are encouraged to do. But this, too, takes time, persistent effort, and vision.

Here, then, are a few moments from "Zion Earth Zen Sky—Learning to Rake," now being considered for publication by the Neal A. Maxwell Institute at Brigham Young University.

*

There are no other Japanese families for miles around. And the nearest Buddhist temple is in Salt Lake City, over two hours north by car. Although my parents want us to have some kind of spiritual training, there are very few possibilities in south-central Utah. Faced with few options, they dress us up every Sunday and take us into Sigurd. They drop us off in front of the Latter-day Saint chapel and come back two hours later to pick us up.

> through the desert air
> comes singing from the chapel—
> knapweed and the moon

My childhood is muffled in the silence of the Utah countryside. I fill the quiet hours alone, wandering outside. Sometimes I play dolls with my sister Annie.

> beyond the wooden fence—
> abandoned trucks, tumbleweeds,
> and bleached deer antlers

Joseph Smith wrote that, as a young man, "left to all kinds of temptations; and, mingling with all kinds of society … [he] frequently fell into many foolish errors … offensive in the sight of God" (JS-H).

I too begin to "mingle with all kinds of society." I too commit "many foolish errors offensive in the sight of God." My weaknesses are legion. But of all my faults, there is one that is particularly troubling.

My brother Dwight points it out to me, "You avoid things. You stay away from people you don't like."

He's right. That's exactly it. Dwight sees me correctly and pointedly, in the way that only an older brother can see a younger brother.

My Aunt Helen, who is also visiting, comes upstairs to comfort me. She puts her arm on my shoulder. She tells me that I'm "a good boy," and that I'll be all right. Her arthritic fingers caress my hair. She stays with me for ten minutes, then goes back downstairs to rejoin the party. I can't stop shaking. Some higher power has knocked me down.

hear the Buddhists say
"there's no such thing as the self"—
sage brush and cedar posts

It doesn't occur to me that my friend Nick would feel so personally hurt by the school board's decision. I doubt he cares. But maybe he does.

That summer, on a warm night in August, just before we go our separate ways, we ride our bikes to the city park and have a long talk about all the things I can't write here. Those kinds of honest conversations don't happen often. When they do, they never let us be the way we once were.

telling the truth
on a warm summer night—
the sound of sprinklers

That final summer begins many dangers for me and my fellow Gunnison Bulldogs. We are hatchery trout, released into a lake filled with bigger fish and surrounded by fishermen with treble hooks and powerbait. Kelly Amtoft gets crushed when his jeep rolls over in the White Hills. David Beck loses his military scholarship when the sleeve of his jacket gets caught in a spinning power-take-off shaft. His arm gets broken into many pieces.

Most of my high school friends go to Utah State, but I decide to attend Brigham Young University. I want to meet people who are smart and believe in god. I need to find a way to deal with how sad the world is.

My freshman year is unusual. Most first-year students live in the dorms, but I share a small rental house with Dwight, Roland Monson, Russell Frandsen, and Dave Hardy. They have all recently returned from their missions.

an icy winter night—
my bicycle slides across
University Ave

After three semesters at BYU, I feel confident enough in my faith to put in an application to go on a mission. A month later, I am called to the Japan Sapporo Mission. I sign the letter and send it back to Salt Lake City. I promise to dedicate myself to the service of others. To show my sincerity, I give up dancing and hunting.

We fly from Salt Lake City to Honolulu, Hawaii. We take a bus to Laie, where we're going to spend the next two months learning Japanese. I am called to be the zone leader of our group of about a sixty people.

> a first test of faith—
> the steepness of the mountains
> is hard to believe

We settle into a strict routine—classes all morning and review sessions in the afternoon and evening. We get an hour a day for exercise and take breaks for meals.

I experience something like "the gift of tongues." It's not that I wake up one morning speaking Nihongo. But I do make unusually quick progress learning a language that is the trunk of one of the tallest and most heralded trees in the forest.

Evening devotionals consist of an opening song, two prayers, and a talk. One of the speakers, I think his name was Brother Honda, gives the same speech three times. Each time, he repeats the same passage of scripture over and over.

> And the Lord called his people Zion, because they were of one heart and one mind, and dwelt in righteousness; and there was no poor among them (Moses 7:18).

"What is Zion?" I wonder. "And why does this guy think it's so important?"

> horned-rim glasses—
> Brother Honda once again
> Zion this and that

Wow, missionary life is even more difficult than farming. Most of our days are spent in a near futile search for investigators. We go from house to house, trying to find someone who is waiting to be taught the gospel. To borrow an idiom from Mencius, it's a little like looking in trees to find fish.

Thank goodness for P-Day (Preparation Day), when we missionaries can take a break from our usual schedule. I am with Shepherd-chōrō, Black-chōrō, and Hirano-chōrō. We take some time off to go see the ocean. We end up in a small cove surrounded by steep cliffs. The beach is stony. We watch the sun set. It envelops us in a golden light, the color of molten copper. The lines between the sky, sea, cliffs, and beach all blur in this profusion. For the first time, I feel the beauty of the sublime.

> round stones on the beach—
> a fishing boat disappears
> into nothingness

I develop a cough. I'm physically exhausted.

Still, I don't want to go home. I can't even imagine what life after my mission will be like.

A month later, my two years are finally over. The plane climbs away from Tokyo and Mt. Fuji disappears in the distance. I finally break down in tears.

Who can possibly understand what I have just been through? The trials, the loneliness, the cold, the hunger, the miracles, the blessings, the lessons learned from raking day after day. People like to make fun of LDS missionaries. But if they took the time to listen to what they have to say, they would learn something astonishing and important—not because the missionaries themselves know all the answers, but because they are "true messengers" of god.

> in my first-class seat—
> the stewardess offers me
> wine but no bread

On the night I return home, the phone rings. Henry has a gun. The Mexicans are afraid he's going to shoot them.

My father insists I stay home and rest. But I put on a coat and go with him to check up on Henry Timican. I've seen him in his drunken rage many times. Before my mission, I even wondered if he might murder my father someday.

We find Henry in his room. We turn on the light.

He's lying on a mattress that glistens with spittle.

My father voices his displeasure. "Why the hell do you have a gun?"

Henry props himself up on an elbow. He yells back in a slurred voice. "To protect *you*, Charlie. If I didn't have a gun, those white boys would steal you blind." By "white boys," he means the local hoodlums who siphon gasoline out of farm trucks and tractors. It happens all the time.

While they talk, I walk around the room. The top drawer of Henry's desk is open. I see his pistol and a box of bullets.

I also notice Henry's two-burner cook stove hissing propane. I click the knob to off.

On the drive back home, the night sky is dark. Behind us, the red of our taillights catches a long contrail of dust that hangs frozen in the winter air. I haven't seen this many stars for two years.

above the mountain's edge
ten billion stars scream—
"You forgot Henry!"

Missionaries are told to forget the world, to focus on the work at hand. But did I go too far? I begin to wonder if my search for purity was just another excuse to separate myself from other people.

As I walk into the house, it dawns on me. The stars in the night sky are justified in their impatience. I've missed the whole point of my mission. In trying to reach perfection by obeying all the rules and working hard, I've been going the wrong direction—not *into* life but *away* from it.

In two years, I've made myself into a pure crystal ball, beautifully disciplined and accomplished. But now I can see that I was trying for the wrong kind of beauty. I've been following the admonition of Saul, not of Paul.

let justice be done!
holding the robes of the
stone throwers

Summer drags on. Charles is miserable. He's not just unhappy. He's depressed. There's something physically wrong with him. He starts getting boils all over his body. He catches a virus and ends up in the hospital.

Life becomes terribly out of balance. Something is missing. Nothing motivates me. None of my goals mean anything anymore. I realize that I have misunderstood god, that I've run out of energy for all the wrong reasons. I was given an opportunity, but I blew it. I realize I have nothing to live for.

A few bad days become a few bad weeks. The spirit leaves me. I am truly alone. I'm horrified to realize I don't believe in anything anymore. It's that simple.

All the things I learned on my mission mean nothing to me now. All the miracles, all the blessings.

I finally understand what hopelessness feels like.

The silence of the Utah countryside moves in. Self-pity takes over. The crew of devils who are assigned to me sense a golden opportunity. "Look at that. Prince Charles has finally worn himself out."

The days drag on. My devils persuade me to end it all. "Why not? What's the point of your meaningless life? What did you think you were going to accomplish anyway?"

I have nothing to say in response.

They're right. Everything is horribly sad. Everything is disappointing. There's really nothing to salvage of the wreck that I've so quickly become. I'm totaled, not worth fixing. Hasn't my homecoming proven that? I've not only missed the point of my mission. I've missed the point of my life.

I pull my shotgun out of its case. I find a shell and push it into the magazine. I lock the round into the firing chamber. I sit on the edge of my bed and take off my shoes.

I click off the safety. I put the barrel to my mouth.

I'm in a trance. I feel the trigger with my big toe. I am about to blow my head off, when I have a thought.

"Look." The spirit breaks through my shell of self-pity and raises a last-minute question. "How sad will your mother and father be if you kill yourself? Can you do that to them? Are you really *that* ungrateful and selfish?"

I put the gun down and eject the shell from the chamber.

"What am I doing?"—
a brass and plastic shotgun shell
rolls on the carpet

Over the next few days, I decide that if I'm going to fix what's wrong with me—if I'm to heal my deep contempt for the world—I need to get out of Utah. Ironically, I'm losing my faith not because I'm too worldly but because I'm not worldly *enough*.

No rich and poor? How can I make Zion happen if I don't know who the rich and the poor are?

I'm pretty confused. But one thing is obvious. I can't go back to BYU. The wide sidewalks and the carefully clipped lawns are comforting. But my path has to take me into the wilderness, not away from it …

Notes

1. Henry Eyring, "O, Remember, Remember," at www.lds.org/general-conference/2007/10/o-remember-remember?lang=eng.

2. D. C. Lau, trans., *Confucius: The Analects* (New York: Dorset Press, 1979), 59.

3. Nishitani Keiji, *Religion and Nothingness,* Jan Van Bragt, trans. (Berkeley: University of California Press, 1982).

4. Charles Inouye, *The End of the World, Plan B* (Salt Lake City: Greg Kofford Books, 2016).

5. Edward Conze, *Buddhist Wisdom: The Diamond Sutra and the Heart Sutra* (New York: Vintage Spiritual Classics, 2001), 86.

6. "God Loved Us So He Sent His Son," text by Edward P. Kimball, music by Alexander Schreiner, in *Hymns of the Church of Jesus Christ of Latter-day Saints* (Salt Lake City: Church of Jesus Christ of Latter-day Saints, 1985), no. 187.

7. The great irony is that the greatest blessings the church affords us are people and ideas we sometimes don't like, as it teaches us not to be comfortable with who we naturally are.

Thirty-Two Variations on an Enduring Theme

Russell M. Frandsen

I have never found it hard to stay in the church. There are three compelling categories of reasons why I stay. Spiritual, experiential or empirical, and rational.

I experience the first, *spiritual*, every month during fast and testimony meeting. On these occasions, I find the witness of the Spirit compelling regarding the atonement of Jesus Christ, the essential truths of the Latter-day Saint understanding of God's purposes, and the essentiality of the ordinances of the gospel. In this essay, I hope to focus on the second and third categories. In doing so, I do not intend to diminish the importance of the first. For me, each intersects with and reinforces the others. I will present thirty-two variations on an enduring theme.

Variation 1. In relation to the *experiential* or *empirical*, my continued participation in the church passes my empirical tests. I have always been attracted to Alma 32. As a farm boy growing up in Gunnison Valley, Utah, whose dream was to be a physicist, I found that Alma provided the perfect paradigm. He suggested that we perform an experiment—an experiment in faith which he likens to planting a seed:

> But behold, if ye will awake and arouse your faculties, even to an experiment upon my words. ... Now, we will compare the word unto a seed. Now, if ye give place, that a seed may be planted in your heart, behold, if it be a true seed, or a good seed, if ye do not cast it out by your unbelief, that ye will resist the Spirit of the Lord, behold, it will begin to swell within your breasts; and when you feel these swelling motions, ye will begin to say within yourselves—It must needs be that this is a good seed, or that

the word is good, for it beginneth to *enlarge my soul*; yea, it beginneth to *enlighten my understanding*, yea, it beginneth to be *delicious to me*. (Alma 32:27–28, emphasis added.)

What have I found to be the empirical results of the experiment that Alma urges us to perform? Generally, I am happier when I am fully participating in the church. My own disposition is sunnier, I am a better friend and spouse, and I approach life and its challenges with optimism and confidence. In addition, I am more entrepreneurial— meaning that I do things intentionally and affirmatively in the spirit of the following modern revelation: "Verily I say, men should be anxiously engaged in a good cause, and do many things of their own free will, and bring to pass much righteousness; For the power is in them, wherein they are agents unto themselves" (D&C 58:27–28).

Variation 2. When I am active in the church, my wife, my children, and I have a happier family life. My wife and I have a better relationship, and we have better relationships with our children. In addition to being less critical of them, I am more accepting of their individual ways of doing things. On a family level, I find the admonition of Doctrine and Covenants 121:41–44 to be perfectly weighted: "No power or influence can or ought to be maintained by virtue of the priesthood, only by persuasion, by long-suffering, by gentleness and meekness, and by love unfeigned; By kindness, and pure knowledge, which shall greatly enlarge the soul without hypocrisy, and without guile."

Variation 3. I find joy in service in the church. I have found fulfillment in all of my callings. Currently, I enjoy working with colleagues in the Stake Young Men's Presidency. I enjoy working on service projects. I even enjoyed my time as Cub Scout den leader and Cub Scout pack master.

Variation 4. I am generally healthier when I am in accordance with the practices of the church. I find the Word of Wisdom to be inspired counsel. I am much healthier than I would be were I a consumer of alcohol and tobacco. I find that my activity in the church encourages an active life style. I have organized a Saturday afternoon soccer game every week, with twenty to thirty participants, ranging from high school and club players, to older players, including former professional players and college players. I enjoy watching the look on high school players faces when they play against me for the first time. They believe they can easily take me on and beat me to the goal and are surprised when they can't!

Variation 5. I do not have any fear of sexually transmitted diseases. Fully faithful Latter-day Saints avoid the risks of worldly lifestyle diseases. I must say, parenthetically, that Latter-day Saints are not immune from debilitating diseases, as I will illustrate below.

Variation 6. The church is a wonderful community. Whenever my family and I have moved into a new ward, we have had instant friends. It takes very little time to establish a web of connections binding us to the ward community.

Variation 7. The church, primarily the local congregations, provides an important support network. In my own life, I have seen it when debilitating sickness occurs. I have seen as recently as when a fire damaged a ward member's house. I have seen it when a young wife dies leaving a husband widowed with three children. I have seen it when a couple in our ward divorces and both partners need support.

Variation 8. Periodic personal priesthood interviews. I find it helpful that members of my family and I have the opportunity to sit down with a priesthood leader to evaluate our commitment to the gospel and involvement in church activities. Personally, I find such opportunities help keep me on track in terms of my stewardship.

Variation 9. The church and its members care enough about me and other members to serve as ministering teachers, to lend support and assistance and provide friendship.

Variation 10. My fellow Saints are "willing to mourn with those that mourn; yea, and comfort those that stand in need of comfort," to quote Mosiah 18:9. The ward members who mourned with us when our five-year-old son succumbed to a central nervous system tumor gave a powerful affirmation of the consoling fellowship abundantly available in the church.

Variation 11. The church is life-affirming. As Latter-day Saints, we affirm the worth of life in general and of each life specifically. We welcome children. I am saddened by the widespread acceptance of abortion for convenience as I am saddened for those who find their lives seemingly pointless.

Variation 12. When I die, I will have a community of Saints who will not only mourn my passing, but celebrate my life as well. I find

Mormon funerals to be truly affirming. I have attended funerals of friends from other faith traditions, even those well respected and known, and find a qualitative difference between them and Latter-day Saint funerals.

Variation 13. Without the church, I would not have the same family I have. I certainly would not have married my wife, Christie. I doubt I would have had eleven children. My life would have been impoverished without them. If I did not stay in the church, I believe these relationships would suffer and something vital would be lost. I would lose a connection with them that is inherent in sharing the faith and hopes in eternity.

Variation 14. I believe Alma's observation that "wickedness never was happiness" (41:10).

Now I would like to turn from the empirical themes that I have just outlined to the third category of reason. I find the following aspects of Mormonism rational justifications for staying.

Variation 15. The church is gender-affirming and gender-valuing. the Latter-day Saints affirm the essential and equal worth of both genders, while also clarifying their different roles in the church and in society. In the temple, women are ordained queens and priestesses, as men are ordained kings and priests. Both genders are essential and neither can achieve God's ultimate purposes alone. I use the term "gender" in the sense of biological sex at birth, although I realize that others use the term "gender" in the sense of social construct encompassing how a person self-identifies. (I do not intend to offend or imply any hidden meanings in my choice of vocabulary, recognizing that the usage and connotation of words change over time, even over short periods of time. I extend tolerance to those who use words differently than I do, and request tolerance for my inartful use of words.) Latter-day Saints have not formulated a satisfying explanation or understanding of homosexuality or gender dysphoria. LGBTQ Latter-day Saints experience real pain in mortality and in contemplating the general Latter-day Saint understanding of life in the resurrection. I believe in the reality of Alma's description of Christ's atonement that "he shall go forth, suffering pains and afflictions and temptations of every kind; and this that the word might be fulfilled which saith he will take upon him the pains and the sicknesses of his people ... that his bowels may be filled with mercy, according to the flesh, that he may know according to the flesh how to succor his people according to their infirmities" (7:11–12). I wish I knew how to give comfort. I believe Christ can give comfort. I believe, however, that LGBTQ Latter-day Saints will have healthier and happier lives by staying close to the Latter-day Saint community and the church than by distancing themselves. I realize that this formulation might not be satisfying to all, but it is my conception at the moment. In all events, I believe that we as Latter-day Saints should always extend the hand of fellowship, inclusion, support, and goodwill to our LGBTQ family members and brothers and sisters in the gospel.

Variation 16. Latter-day Saints insist upon personal responsibility. I find this particularly invigorating.

Variation 17. Latter-day Saints insist upon compassion. I find this a powerful well-spring of humanitarianism.

Variation 18. The Latter-day Saints' gospel requires consecration. I find this to be a powerful preventative to selfishness and narcissism.

Variation 19. I rejoice in the lack of creeds and orthodoxy. We have much less to answer for as a church because we have no formal creeds. We have much more freedom of thought and practice. When we as members take non-canonical past statements of prominent leaders as creeds, rather than as pastoral teachings, we get into trouble, as our racialist history shows.

Variation 20. I find the LDS conception of God and his relationship to us to be ennobling for us, not denigrating of God. I find it reasonable that we are made in the image of God.

Variation 21. I believe that the doctrine of deification gives purpose and rationale to our lives.

Variation 22. I believe it is reasonable that God is subject to laws, as LDS scripture affirms. This means that God is not arbitrary. We can have faith in God because he will not act arbitrarily.

Variation 23. I believe it is reasonable that we are co-existent with God and therefore have ultimate meaning and existence alongside God.

Variation 24. I believe the Book of Mormon is a powerful affirmation for staying in the church. I have asked the question whether the Book of Mormon is our boon or our bane. To me, it is a boon, although I realize to others it might be a bane. In my view, most of the attacks on the Book of Mormon have been attacks on its origin and the process of its translation and publication. One recent attack concerns disputes over DNA evidence. With this and other issues, questions still linger without fully satisfactory answers; but given the progress over time in addressing Book of Mormon questions, I am willing to grant additional time for the accumulating corroborating evidence.

Variation 25. As a committed Latter-day Saint, I believe that I must also contend with the unpleasant and the disturbing threads in the fabric of the church and its history. I use the term church to include the people, their attitudes, and widespread beliefs. First and foremost is our racialist history. (I prefer the term "racialist" to "racist" because generally I have found that Latter-day Saints had true feelings of good will toward all races and looked forward to the end of the priesthood and temple restrictions.) I simply reject the policy prior to 1978 as tragically mistaken and the teachings and folklore that supported the policy as distorted rationalizations with their origins in Anglo-American justifications of slavery. However, I do not expect perfection of either church leaders or my fellow saints. Paul said that "we see through a glass darkly" (1 Cor. 13:12). Joseph Smith said that God speaks to the Saints in their "weakness, after the manner of their language" (D&C 1:24). I recognize that our human frailties, mine included, are part of our mortal experience. Nevertheless, we must apologize and do our best to rectify the damage that the church in this broad sense has inflicted.

Variation 26. I see conflicts with generally accepted doctrines of the church and some current scientific theories. In particular, the conclusions that some draw from what they perceive as chaos and randomness seem to conflict with the notion of a divine hand acting in nature. We have become so enamored of science and technology in our day that we attribute a certainty to contemporary scientific theories that I think may be undeserved. The history of science has been a history of radical overturning of scientific orthodoxy. I expect this to continue. I do think we are making scientific progress. Even the positing of scientific explanations that prove entirely unsatisfactory can move us forward by stimulating a new set of responses or perspectives. I applaud our scientific and technological progress. However, I think we need humility in accepting the finality of contemporary scientific explanations.

Variation 27. I see conflicts with trends in secularism and elite culture. I believe we should accept the good aspects we see in secularism, but I also believe we should have the same skepticism toward secularism and elite culture that I have described in relationship to science and technology.

Variation 28. I have had to confront the problem of theodicy, both personally and philosophically. Theodicy actually means the justification of God, but it has come to mean the problem of evil or suffering existing in the world that is supposedly governed by a benevolent God. What do I say personally when my own five-year-old son dies of a central nervous system tumor, or my youngest child dies at birth, my thirty-one-year-old daughter with a husband and three small children becomes materially debilitated by multiple sclerosis, and my brother undergoes the terminal stages of Lou Gehrig's disease? What do I say when my prayers for relief are not answered in the way that I would have them answered? What do I say to the suffering of children and others in war and poverty? I do not think we can condemn God for either creating the suffering, misery and atrocities or for not eliminating them. I do not believe that such things constitute evidence that God does not exist or that he is not a benevolent God. As a Latter-day Saint, I reject the notion that God has the power to either foreclose suffering and evil or to necessarily relieve them. God is subject to laws and can only do that which natural law allows. Because he respects the agency of human beings, God cannot arbitrarily proscribe that agency. Since I believe that natural laws are co-eternal with God, I cannot blame God for these natural laws from which evil, suffering, and misery follow as consequences of their operation.

Variation 29. Where would I go? If I were to leave the church, where would I go? To other Christian churches? While I would find much good there, would I find the type of "empirical" or "experiential" validation that I find within the church? I do not believe so. Would I go to other world religions? I do not find that appealing in light of the variations that I have described above. Would I go to agnosticism and/ or atheism? I do not believe the evidence points to our existence as random or meaningless. I have nowhere else to go.

Variation 30. What do I lose or foreclose by staying within the church, or, phrased differently, what would I gain by leaving the church? I would gain more free time. Would I use it any more meaningfully? I would gain a certain sociality, typified by sharing a glass of wine at dinner or coffee at Starbucks in a setting of authentic conviviality. Could that replace the community I find within the church? I would gain a 15 percent increase in disposable income. I could name others. Yet I find that these factors do not weigh heavy in the scales of my belief.

Variation 31. Although I am familiar with the critiques of Pascal's Wager, I find it convincing:

> "God is, or He is not." But to which side shall we incline? Reason can decide nothing here. ... Which will you choose then? ... Since you must choose, let us see which interests you least. ... Your reason is no more shocked in choosing one rather than the other, since you must of necessity choose. ... But your happiness? Let us weigh the gain and the loss in wagering that God is. ... If you gain, you gain all; if you lose, you lose nothing. Wager, then, without hesitation that He is. (See www.seop.leeds. ac.uk/entries/pascal-wager.)

I like to apply this same logic to the church. Since I view the practices and teachings of the church as at least as honorable (even if more eccentric) than other religious alternatives, and more so than secular, agnostic and atheistic choices, I lose nothing by staying in the church. But if the church is the only true and living church of God, then I gain all.

Variation 32. Finally, I believe in intellectual and spiritual humility in the context of all that we do not know and the uncertainties that we confront. I take comfort in the following beautiful words of Isaiah 55:1–3, 8–13:

> Ho, every one that thirsteth, come ye to the waters, and he that hath no money; come ye, buy, and eat; yea, come, buy wine and milk without money and without price. ... Incline your ear, and come unto me: hear, and your soul shall live; and I will make an everlasting covenant with you, even the sure mercies of David. ... For my thoughts are not your thoughts, neither are your ways my ways, saith the Lord. For as the heavens are higher than the earth, so are my ways higher than your ways, and my thoughts than your thoughts. For as the rain cometh down, and the snow from heaven, and returneth not thither, but watereth the earth, and maketh it bring forth and bud, that it may give seed to the sower, and bread to the eater: So shall my word be that goeth forth out of my mouth: it shall not return unto me void, but it shall accomplish that which I please, and it shall prosper in the thing whereto I sent it. For ye shall go out with joy, and be led forth with peace: the mountains and the hills shall break forth

before you into singing, and all the trees of the field shall clap their hands. Instead of the thorn shall come up the fir tree, and instead of the brier shall come up the myrtle tree: and it shall be to the Lord for a name, for an everlasting sign that shall not be cut off.

Perhaps when I am at the end of my life, I will be able to say why I stayed a member of the Church of Jesus Christ of Latter-day Saints, but these are the reasons I choose to stay today.

God Values the Sincere Pursuit of Truth and Goodness

Jennifer Finlayson-Fife

I grew up as a member of the church in Burlington, Vermont, in the 1970s and 1980s. Church membership in New England was very sparse at the time, and my parents, having transplanted from the Intermountain West, were essential to its functioning in our community. They held multiple callings in the branch and district, frequently invited members to our home for dinners and firesides, assisted the missionaries, and even helped to build the chapel. Because our family life revolved around our belief and participation, our membership in the church was *everything* to us.

Not only were we needed in our small branch, but we also experienced the outside world as foreign—even unsafe—living as we did amidst gentiles. We saw ourselves as part of a chosen people, but also a misunderstood and persecuted people. And in this perception, I found security and comfort in my affiliation with other church members. Additionally, Primary and Young Women's leaders cared about me and mentored me. I knew that I mattered to my congregation and that we needed one another. These experiences forged in me a strong sense of community and identity as a Latter-day Saint. Given my strong identification, I trusted the testimonies and teachings of my parents and leaders regarding who I was and who I should become—as a Mormon, as a disciple of Christ, and as a female.

I learned at a young age that I had a heavenly father who knew and loved me. I believed that reality deeply and carried it in my heart. It was a tangible source of comfort for me. The gospel gave me a framework for making sense of my existence and a strong sense of purpose within it. I learned the concepts of self-mastery and eternal progression. And I identified with the idea that I was a daughter of God, had divine potential, and that my choices mattered. Even though the path was challenging, it was meaningful and I felt I was chosen for it. These beliefs blessed my life, and I continue to be grateful for the ways that our theology created vision and resiliency within me.

But at a young age I also perceived that I lived in a man's world and recognized that my mother knew this too. This was a given—something that shaped and defined our reality as Latter-day Saint women. My family structure strongly resembled the church's idealized notions of gender: My father was the breadwinner, a leader in the home and in the church, the more dominant personality, and the primary decision-maker in our family. He embodied the best in patriarchy in that he took seriously and lived up to his responsibilities as a leader and provider. My mother was warm-hearted, patient, and deferential, in reality, the embodiment of the Mormon woman ideal: She was beautiful, domestically skilled, and loved her faith and her children deeply.

Living in a world where men lead and women followed did not mean I was devalued. I was openly cherished by my parents as their first daughter, following the births of my four older brothers. I was seen as a gift from God to my family (in particular to my mother—who saw me as a friend and female ally). And although it was clear to me that women were valued and what we contributed mattered, I also understood that God was male and that boys and men, through the bestowal of the priesthood, had God's trust in a way that women did not. Priesthood-bearing men had greater access to God's wisdom and were therefore divinely appointed to direct women. Furthermore, as an adolescent, I learned that polygamy was considered the highest form of marriage in the next life, that being someone's wife and someone's mother were my loftiest aspirations, and that any sexual behavior outside of marriage would interfere with achieving the status of being desired by a priesthood holder.

So I mattered, but as a female I also understood that I was condescended to. Women were supports to men and children first and individuals second. While I was very happy to be female and loved the church and the foundation it offered me, I was deeply ambivalent about embracing my mother's position relative to a mate. I saw her lower status in her marriage and in the church, and I saw her dependency on both for a sense of self. I also witnessed her feelings of inadequacy relative to my father's influence and education. Most painful for me was the divine sanction for this reality. This was a very real source of doubt and personal anguish. This theology felt wrong, yet I feared it was right. And this drove some ambivalence into my heart about my identification with the church.

Additionally, I was, from a very young age, a thinker and a questioner. I wanted to have a testimony like my leaders and peers, but I had difficulty seeing the church as the simple source for God's will and authority on earth. While I had a strong conviction of many of the church's teachings and considered them invaluable, I was not able to let go of doubts about teachings that were incongruent with my notions of fairness and of a compassionate God. I wanted to be an unambiguous believer because it was so essential to belonging, and belonging to my religious group mattered very much to me. However, despite reading the Book of Mormon, praying daily, reading scriptures regularly, and taking my faith very seriously, I wasn't able to gain a witness from God in the way others claimed to.

At age eighteen, I left home to attend Brigham Young University where my questions increased. A few people close to me shared their difficulties with faith given their discovery of challenging historical realities and questions about the authenticity of scriptural texts. Even though I couldn't make sense of these issues either, I chose to persevere in faith and hoped that perhaps my ongoing doubt and lack of a witness was a function of my spiritual immaturity, not the veracity of the church. At twenty-one, I chose to serve a mission, both as an expression of devotion and as a sacrifice before God. I would give my very best as a missionary and learn all I could about the gospel in the hope of finally receiving a witness of the divinity of the church. Serving in Spain, I put all of my doubts and questions aside, trusted in the missionary program, and worked whole-heartedly. While functioning in that relatively closed and self-reinforcing system, my belief and confidence in the gospel increased. However, toward the end of my mission, that protective shield was punctured when I received a long letter from my best friend who explained in great detail why she could no longer believe in the church, and why, instead of going on a mission herself, she was leaving the faith.

Reading my friend's letter, all of my doubts and questions returned, no more reconciled or resolved than they had been prior to my mission. In spite of myself, I understood and identified with her disbelief. Nevertheless, I was desperate to resolve the matter in my own heart and plead with God to grant me a testimony. With great earnestness, I fasted and prayed for two days then continued to pray and to write in my journal with an unprecedented intensity. I couldn't live with the dissonance any longer. On the fourth day, I received what I believe was an answer from God: It was Holy Week (or *Semana Santa*) in Spain, and while watching a procession with gilded religious figurines, I had a strong impression that, using language from Joseph Smith's epistle to the church in 1842, seemed "to occupy my mind, and press itself upon my feelings" (D&C 128:1)—"Jennifer, there are false traditions everywhere. No individual or entity can give you all of the answers. It is your job to sort out in your own heart what is true from what is false, and live by what you honestly believe is true." I knew in my heart that I had received an answer and that it was right. I felt known by God and I felt relief that I had a direction to move forward without the anguish of trying to make something entirely right that for me wasn't entirely right. But reflecting on the answer, I also felt afraid—afraid to live by my honest sense of right and wrong because I knew I would not agree with all aspects of accepted doctrine. I would not bear witness of things of which I lacked conviction, but I was afraid of the social cost of living with greater integrity.

I wanted the respect of members of the church; I wanted to belong as a Latter-day Saint, and yet I knew if I were to speak openly about the problems I saw in our theology and practice, I would lose status, if not my membership. I had fear and later anger about this. Fear, because I was afraid to lose the approval of those who matter most to me, and anger, because the expected beliefs of my faith community forced me to experience an unwanted dilemma: I could either belong to the community that I loved or belong to myself, but I did not see how I could do both. My desire for the validation of family and friends pressured me into the pretense of orthodoxy and I resented it. I coped by being critical and at times superior to ostensibly unquestioning members, even if I engaged in this silently. With time, I recognized that my un-willingness to risk greater authenticity increased my hostility toward the church because it was antithetical to my desire to be a kind and courageous person. I eventually gave myself permission to leave the church if I needed to and to face the social consequences that might follow in living more honestly.

But with the internal freedom to go, my desire to stay soon became evident. Shortly after distancing myself from the church, it became clear that I cared too much about my religious community to willfully disconnect from it. The church was my family; Latter-day Saints were my people. They had cared for and invested in me since I was a young child. And I wanted to find a way to authentically be a part of my peo-ple, even if it meant rejection. I also recognized that as a truth-seeking member, I was a legitimate Latter-day Saint, and I was determined not to allow differences in understanding about what constituted truth to take away that central identity. And so I no longer accepted that my unorthodox voice was an inferior one, or that it was a threatening one in the cause of goodness, even if some thought so.

Because in my core convictions, I believe in a God who is greater than all of our ideas about God. And I believe in a God who val-ues integrity and the pursuit of truth over blind obedience or rigid conformity. I am certain that many of my most heartfelt beliefs and perspectives are incorrect or limited, but I believe God values the sin-cere pursuit of truth and goodness even when I am wrong.

While most of us take comfort in similarities, it is in grappling honestly with divergent experiences that we are led to develop greater compassion for one another and discover greater truth. Joseph Smith said, "By proving contraries, truth is made manifest."[1] And, as Paul said about the body of Christ, no member of that body can say to one another, "I have no need of thee" (1 Cor. 12:21). Having to respond to a brother or sister's pain challenges us to become a wiser and more God-like people. Christ modeled this over and over—compassion is more important than strict adherence to ideology.

I have found the courage to stay and invest in my religious com-munity because of my confidence that creating the body of Christ is not a top-down endeavor and not an exclusively obedience-driven en-deavor. Instead, in creating the body of Christ, a godly people is forged through communal striving to live according to earnestly sought truth and through love for one another. This ideal gives me confidence to learn from others, including leaders, and then stand for what I honestly believe. It gives me courage to invest in my Mormon people. I want to live up to the best in Mormonism and stand for the goodness in it and not allow false traditions to be given gospel status. I am grateful for all that this community of believers has given to me, and I choose to stay in the moral conversation and invest in return. This is why I stay.

Notes

1. In Joseph Smith et al., *History of the Church of Jesus Christ of Latter-day Saints* (Salt Lake City: Deseret Book Co., 1970), 6:428.

Where God Is: A Widening View

Carol Lynn Pearson

Years ago when my husband, Gerald, and I made the outrageous decision to self-publish my poems, I wrote this simple piece that became the title poem of one of the books:

A Widening View

When my eye first opened
Behind the viewfinder,
There, in closeup,
Was a flower—
The only possible flower.

Who turned the lens
For the pullback?
Life, I guess.
What—
Another flower?
And another?
A field alive with flowers?
(The only possible field?)

Loss.
Delight.

Borders are forever gone.
Life is at the lens.
The view goes on
And on.

George Bernard Shaw said it better in *Major Barbara:* "You have learned something. That always feels at first as if you have lost something."

I was born in Salt Lake City, fourth-generation Mormon, ancestors having come variously by wagon train, on the ship *Brooklyn,* and with the Mormon Battalion. I was planted firmly in the LDS corner of the vineyard with the Mormon flower the only one in sight.

And then came the pullback. The intriguing beauty of all the other flowers. How could it be—with the grand diversity of this splendid field—that mine is the one true flower? Examining it carefully, decades ago in my thirties and forties, I found that to my eyes (and who else's eyes could I possibly use, even though mine see through a glass darkly?) there were some pretty evident flaws—historical and doctrinal positions that seemed indefensible and that felt wrong. Many today who come to feel that way find it highly distressing. I found it thrilling. I gained a new respect for God, a new delight in every one of the billions who inhabit this planet. And, having given up impossible expectations, I gained a new affection and appreciation for this particular flower—mine—and yours.

"Grow where you are planted." I expect that is what the Dalai Lama meant when he said that whenever possible we should stay in the religion we were born to. Many of my friends from my BYU days—especially women friends—have left Mormondom, have transplanted themselves to different ground. In general, I see them thriving. And so the question arises, why do I stay?

There are two very large reasons. One—I find a great deal of love in this church. Two—where I do not find love, I have an opportunity to help create love.

Reason Number One. I have confessed to my ward and stake leadership that my theology comes down to "God is love," as illustrated in the little song that we sing, "Where Love Is, There God Is Also." To me this means wherever in a straight or a gay relationship there is genuine caring and devotion—there God is. And where in Islam, in Catholicism, in Buddhism, in Mormonism there is genuine caring and devotion—there God is. The fact of the matter is that in Mormonism I find a great deal of love—and therefore a great deal of God.

Too many people are alone in our world today. What a blessing to have a large ward family and even a worldwide family. Out to see the world after saving my money teaching at Snow College in Ephraim, Utah, for a year, I arrived in Athens, Greece, on my twenty-fourth birthday to realize that my luggage had been stolen from the train and I had only my passport, my purse, and what I was wearing. I made one phone call—to the nearby US Air Force base to ask for the Mormons. I was not entirely naked, but they clothed me. I was hungry, and they fed me. I was a stranger, and they took me in. We give, and we take. We call each other brother and sister. We have a system. It is quite remarkable.

Sunday before last as I arrived at our chapel, I saw an ambulance pulling in. It was there for Susan, who has had seizures since she was six years old. This time she hit her head on the concrete in the parking lot. I had been Susan's visiting teacher for many years, and I knew her needs well. I was the obvious choice to volunteer to drive with her in the ambulance and to stay with her through the tests in the hospital, rubbing her feet and talking and even laughing. It was easy. We have a system. I was her sister.

I wrote in my book *Goodbye, I Love You*, the story of when Sister Spencer, my visiting teacher at the time, called me, having been given the information that I was caring for my former husband as he was dying. She said, "I'm not calling to ask if I can do anything for you. I'm calling to tell you to put a pen and a notebook by your phone, and whenever anything occurs to you that needs to be done, write it down. I will call at nine each morning and you will read me the list and the things will be done." A wonderful gift. We had a system. She was my sister. Sort of sounds like … Zion.

A few years ago I happened to be sitting beside my friend Chuck Young in sacrament meeting, listening to our high council speaker, who is now our stake president. I leaned over and whispered, "Chuck, you know what really pisses me off about the Mormon patriarchy?"

"What?" he whispered back.

"That it continues to create such really fine men. Like you and Brother Criddle up there."

My Mormon life is populated with good men. And certainly with good women. Much love there. Much of God there.

Reason Number Two. Our church provides a perfect opportunity for me to create love in places where it appears to be lacking. I think creating more love in the world is the only reason to try to change anything. I was born a feminist, asking questions by the time I was ten, amazed that every voice of authority—from the voices on the radio to the voices at church to the voice of God—was a male voice. I was outraged that by every measure in church and society femaleness was second prize. There's no love in that.

Last Sunday I sang with the congregation the beautiful hymn, "We'll Sing All Hail to Jesus' Name," and in the midst of eight pronouns honoring masculine divinity, there was only one feminine pronoun: "The grave yield up her dead." There is no love in that, and the insult is not lost on the psyches of women and men, boys and girls who sing it. Of course I sang, "The grave yield up *its* dead."

Not long ago I asked a dear cousin who is in her nineties how she felt about going to the next world. "Fine," she said, "Except ...," and her face clouded, "... except sometimes I worry that my husband has taken a second wife over there." There is no love in that. We should be ashamed. And I have only started the long list of things we need to look at for us to achieve equal valuing—meaning equal love—for women as well as men.

I came home from church last Sunday to find six emails, most from people who felt they needed to connect with me on gay issues. A man speaking of his dearly loved teenage son wrote, "He has told us several times that there have been times he wanted to take his life, because he was 'going to hell' anyway." The father continues, "I understand this feeling. I am somewhat going through this as well. The more I read my scriptures and say my prayers, the more I think about him and get depressed." There is no love in what we are putting that family through. Our church is utterly failing them and thousands of families like them, and we ought to be ashamed. I looked for the love in our church's work for Proposition 8 (California) and I found none. I have found love in the groundswell of support for our gay brothers and sisters—such as the remarkable photographs of 400 Mormons in their Sunday best marching at the front of Salt Lake City's gay pride parade. Some of the spectators who wept while they watched knew there was love there. I am moved at the increasing number of stories gay people are sharing of warm, encouraging conversations with their ward and stake leaders. We all know love when we see it and feel it. We can't be tricked.

We have the privilege in our day of doing something of historical importance for our gay loved ones just as our ancestors did when they gave up the slave trade, when they banned segregation, when they decided women had souls and even gave them the vote. They knew there was no love in what they had been doing and also knew that for there to be love things had to change. You and I have the privilege of seeing the sad places and creating more love—more goodness—more godness.

Circumstance has given me a platform and a voice at a time and in a place where significant impact can be made. We are preparing in society, in religion and, yes, in our own church to invite our gay brothers and sisters, as individuals and as couples and families, to take an honored place at the table. Amazing. And eventually we will get around to creating a Galileo moment when we cease to see maleness as the center of the universe with femaleness orbiting around it, but instead see male and female—mortal and divine—doing a dance of true partnership. I would not for anything give up being part of the action. Right now. Right here. In this particular, peculiar—unique in its own way, and wonderful in many ways—Mormon corner of the Lord's vast vineyard.

I stay because not only am I allowed to stay, but because I feel very appreciated. Now and then I speak to my bishop or my stake presidency and say, "Brethren, again I want to thank you for being so gracious to someone like me who does not fit the mold." Always, I receive some form of this reply, "Sister Pearson, we are so grateful for the wonderful contributions you make to our ward and stake." In Relief Society I stand up when I make my comments, and if I'm absent for more than two Sundays, I might receive an email from one of the sisters saying, "Are you okay? We miss your comments in Relief Society."

I also believe an important reason that I am able to stay is that in some ways I do not stay. I do not stay in concepts that I do not accept. I do not stay in traditions that I do not believe in. I move, in my own very imperfect way, toward the horizon that truly calls to me. I believe the best thing I received from my pioneer ancestors was not a destination, but an invitation. They gave me the model of being a pioneer and encouraged me to follow in their footsteps.

Perhaps, finally, the following poem of mine dramatizes why and how I stay and pull up stakes at the same time:

Pioneers

My people were Mormon pioneers.
Is the blood still good?
They stood in awe as truth
Flew by like a dove
And dropped a feather in the West.
If you are a pioneer.

I have searched the skies
And now and then
Another feather has fallen.
I have packed the handcart again
Packed it with the precious things
And thrown away the rest.

I will sing by the fires at night
Out there on uncharted ground
Where I am my own captain of tens
Where I blow the bugle
Bring myself to morning prayer
Map out the miles
And never know when or where
Or if at all
I will finally say,
"This is the place."

I face the plains
On a good day for walking.
The sun rises
And the mist clears.

I will be all right.
My people were Mormon pioneers.

Staying Takes Work

Mitch Mayne

As an openly gay Mormon, I've been asked many times by well-intentioned friends and acquaintances, "Why don't you just leave the church?" It is an understandable question. In one sense, leaving might actually seem an easier option than staying engaged in a faith tradition where I am often viewed as "The Other."

But the question overlooks something critical and unique to Mormonism. Being Mormon isn't simply something we practice for an hour on Christmas and Easter. It's not even something we practice for three hours each Sunday. Mormonism isn't merely a religion—it is also a culture, and one that deeply embeds itself into who we are as humans.

Being Mormon affects what we eat, what we drink, what clothes we wear, what movies we see, and how we spend our money and our time. It often affects whether or not we go to college and which universities we choose to attend, and then, ultimately, what careers we choose. It most certainly affects the significance we place on relationships—especially to those with whom we are the closest—our families, friends, and, when we're lucky, our partners.

Being Mormon embeds itself not only into our daily lives, but also into what I call our *spiritual DNA*—impacting the kind of humans we become. When we leave our religion (and our culture) behind, whether by choice or by factors beyond our control, it often leaves a hole in our identity.

But staying inside a faith with such a deep and rich (and sometimes rigid and frustrating) culture when you don't fit the traditional mold is sometimes a tricky thing. It takes work—real emotional and spiritual work—to remain committed to an organization when the message you sometimes hear from your fellow believers is, "You don't belong here."

There are many reasons *why* I stay. But I want to focus on something that we don't often talk about inside our faith: *how* I stay. I want to look at the fundamentals and principles that allow me to navigate a religion into which, at least on the surface, I don't seem to fit.

How I Stay

I'm able to stay because I understand there is a distinct difference between the Church of Jesus Christ of Latter-day Saints and my Savior on whom I have built my faith and to whom I have given my primary allegiance.

Placing my faith in the institution instead of in Christ is a bit like putting my faith in the sales team, not the product. By recognizing and placing faith in my Savior—where, I believe, it rightly belongs—I have allowed myself to let go of many unrealistic expectations I once had of my religion. And, as a friend once told me, an expectation is nothing more than a premeditated resentment.

I no longer expect my church, its leaders, or its members to be perfect—including me. I don't expect my church to be a leading authority on science, politics, nutrition, or any other subject. Instead, I recognize it for what it is intended to be: one of many spiritual pathways to our Lord. When I expect the church to be a leading authority on other subjects—like LGBT issues, for example—in essence, I set both of us up for failure. I have learned that expecting my church to be an expert on all things is akin to going to the hardware store for bread: they cannot supply what they do not have.

Conversely, I understand that my Savior *is* perfect, and it is through him and the privilege of personal revelation and salvation that I am able to negotiate my path in life, including my life in the church.

When I let go of unrealistic expectations of others, I allow them to be free to make errors, to stumble and to learn, grow, and progress as participants in our heavenly parents' plan. I allow them to focus on their own salvation—rather than expecting them to manage mine. That, in turn, allows me to be free from carrying around the unnecessary burden of resentments toward others who—while perhaps well intentioned—may not know what is right for me.

I'm able to stay because I have developed a deep and personal relationship with my Lord by cultivating a rich spiritual practice—comprised of both Mormon traditions and practices from other faiths.

I think of this as "diversifying my spiritual portfolio."

When we invest in our 401(k), we're taught to diversify our investments both to mitigate risk (in case one investment fails) and to reap bigger rewards (by casting a wider net to include stocks and bonds that may increase in value). This same principle applies to us spiritually. When we cast a wide net, we discover our Savior is all around us. Some of us find him in nature, others in meditation, and still others in our Mormon scriptures or the texts of other faiths. We learn he does not hide himself from us but can be found in a myriad of places and accessed in many different ways.

Because my spiritual practice is both broad and deep, I find I can make time to engage in some part of it each day. Whether through silent prayer, in meditation, or through journaling, I'm able to connect with my Savior in some small way each day. This method of frequent contact stretches me both spiritually and emotionally. I find when I make time for spiritual contact—no matter how small—I become more humble, more grateful, and more gentle with others. And ultimately, this moves me closer to the kind of person both God and I want me to be.

I'm able to stay because I recognize that I am the one who is responsible for my spiritual well-being.

One of the enlightened teachings of the restored gospel is that we all have both the gift and the responsibility of personal revelation and guidance. As Mormons, we sometimes think this concept—personal relationship with Christ and the guidance that comes from it—is something we can (or should) abdicate. But we cannot and should not abdicate that right and responsibility to anyone, independent of his or her position or role in our lives. To do so places an unnecessary and inappropriate burden on another and removes us from the direct and powerful insight we are both in need of and obligated to acquire.

But what, exactly, is my responsibility and what belongs to others? A friend used the selection of a Hula-Hoop as a metaphor When you select a Hula-Hoop, it's important to understand that size matters. The correctly sized Hula-Hoop for you is one that will give you about twelve inches of room all the way around if you stand in the center. Within that space, advised my friend, fall the things for which I am primarily responsible—and it is where my spiritual serenity and peace lie. Everything that falls outside that space (with some small exceptions, which I will cover in a moment) is either of secondary importance or not my business at all.

Within my circle, I am responsible for the following: ensuring my spiritual well-being and building my relationship with Christ; understanding and being loyal to my values; keeping an open mind and a soft heart; ridding myself of anger and resentment; expressing my feelings and ideas instead of denying or repressing them; being realistic with my expectations of myself and others; making emotionally, spiritually, and physically healthy choices for myself; and being grateful for my blessings.

I also have some responsibility to those outside that circle: to extend kindness and welcome to any who cross my path; to be of service to my Savior and others; to recognize that others have the right to live their lives and allowing them the dignity to do so; to listen—not just with my ears, but with my heart; to share my joy as well as my sorrow; and, most important, to treat all others with kindness, gentleness, and love.

And I know that I can attend to things beyond my circle *only after* I have taken care of those things that lie within it.

I'm able to stay because I'm no longer in the business of living other people's version of my life.

As a gay Mormon, I have many well-meaning friends and acquaintances both inside and outside the church (and everywhere in between) who are not hesitant to tell me how I should live my life. Most days, it seems I can't be Mormon enough for my LDS community, and I can't be gay enough for my LGBT fellows.

I've discovered it's not possible for me to become the best person my heavenly parents intended me to be if I'm always putting someone else's ideas of how to live above my own—or above my Savior's. This has required (and, in some ways, enabled) me to put into place a solid set of spiritual and emotional boundaries, and to understand keenly where I leave off and others begin.

I don't want to be misunderstood: Seeking counsel from wise and trusted friends is always a good thing—and I avail myself of that privilege frequently. But I also listen critically and have learned that there is a difference between those who share their own experience and testimony and those who want to dictate choices for me. I recognize the former when people speak from the heart and share what they've learned along their paths. I recognize the latter because it generally comes in the form of sentences that begin with phrases like, "You need to," "You should," or "You must."

When I hear sentences that begin with these kinds of phrases, I know I've crossed from hearing someone's experience and wisdom into the realm of hearing their opinion. When that happens, I gently thank them but also remind myself that the only opinion of me that really matters more than my own is that of my Savior. As someone once said, "What other people think of me is none of my business."

These are some of the fundamental philosophies that underpin *how I stay*. Underneath all of this is my conviction that every single one of us is equal in the eyes of our heavenly parents and our Savior regardless of ethnicity, gender, sexual orientation, or any other marker we use to define differences between ourselves and others.

As a member of this human family, I don't believe it is ever my job to condemn, criticize, or mock another. My job, as one of God's sons, is to walk beside you as you learn the lessons life is intended to teach you; to celebrate your joys with you; and to lend a hand when you stumble. The true spirit of love we have for one another is kind, patient, and doesn't demand its own way. It doesn't scold, condemn, or criticize.

I am most certainly an imperfect human—but this is the spirit I think our Savior wants us to strive to achieve as his children and as brothers and sisters. It is the spirit that I endeavor to bring to my entire life—and most certainly my faith.

Allegiance, Affinity, and Affection

Emma Lou Warner Thayne

> "Seek not to counsel life, but to take counsel from its hand."
> —Jacob 4:12

Oh, the counseling of life! Nothing is less linear than memory, more complicated in its emergence. In that silvery configuration of remembering, I have gratefully come to know much more about why I am a Mormon. I love it. Any problems I have with the church are with organizational matters, not with believing. Three A's define my staying: Allegiance, Affinity, and Affection.

First, *Allegiance*. Mormonism is my heritage, beginning with my great-grandfather. Great-grandfather Willard Richards was at Carthage Jail, Illinois, that fateful day when the Prophet Joseph Smith was killed. He offered to give his life to save Joseph's. Imagine his heartbreak. When he took the sorrowful news back to his fellow saints in Nauvoo, he responded not with feelings of revenge, but, as Joseph had taught him, peace. After emigrating to the Great Basin, he became the first editor of the *Deseret News* as well as a doctor/healer. That conviction of peace and healing, not retribution and war, is in my genes.

I also love the idea of a visionary background on which the church was founded, believing that God is still available, not only to prophets who can change precepts like polygamy or priesthood to Blacks when expedient, but on a personal level, to anyone willing to ask and to listen to promptings of the Spirit.

What explains my commitment to the church but allegiance to that kind of pioneer steadfastness and optimism? It is part of my heritage; I grew up imbibing peace in a home of joy and expectation of good. Ours was not a religion of rules and edicts superimposed upon life, but life itself—life from an eternal standpoint; life from God's point of view. Belonging meant reverence for life in great variety, reverence for the kitchen and the canyon, for a family picnic and Bible stories read by Mother and Father, for throwing a ball or playing with jacks and dolls.

My father, having lost his car business, had to travel as a Lincoln automobile division manager, but he and Mother wrote to one another every day and lent their unique outlooks to our becoming. We never knew we were poor and relished a penny to spend at the confectionary as if we were millionaires.

Always accenting the positive, Father's motto was from athletics and initiating the churchwide M-Men basketball program—"Try hard, play fair, and have fun." He made it all look appealing, not only on the court but in life. The motto of our mother, our aesthetic poet and painter, was, "Pray at night, plan in the morning." Her faith was grounded in something as simple and practical as our growing up healthy by eating her oatmeal for breakfast. She was not a scriptorian but considered prayers, fasting, and blessings as both natural and guaranteed to provide healing like dew from heaven. Of my three brothers, Homer, Rick, and Gill, only Gill went on a mission. My husband-to-be, Mel, didn't serve a mission either, but all of them were married in the temple and later became bishops. As attuned as we were to our heritage, we never felt our church had a corner on happy families or goodness. We grew up finding both all around us.

Then there is *Affinity*, the ineffable of being drawn to what can't be willed or willed away. Affinity began for me in the high-ceilinged, English Tudor Highland Park Ward, my church home for the twenty-five years before I was married. Here religion was also basic and practical. Hung in perfect view, two framed ovals set the pattern of my believing: high in the back of the chapel, "*The glory of God is intelligence,*" and in the most occupied anteroom "*Man is that he might have joy.*" What more sturdy invitations to a life rich in questing?

As I hear more complicated formulas for faith recited near and far, and warnings about the dreary world and the Adversary, the old fashioned in me still remembers the Beehive Creed I learned at twelve: *Have faith, seek knowledge, honor womanhood, taste the sweetness of service, love* one another—simple and lasting as the words to "I Know that My Redeemer Lives" or "For the Strength of the Hills" sung with the fervor of belonging. Or the Articles of Faith memorized and internalized like the Word of Wisdom, especially the first, incorporated not as "we" believe, but "I" *believe in God the eternal Father and in his son Jesus Christ, and in the Holy Ghost*, and on to the 13th—*to endure and hope and to seek after anything virtuous, lovely, of good report or praiseworthy.*

Also sitting for all those years in Highland Park Ward engendered in me a great affinity for Joseph Smith, as real as the Lee Greene Richards's painting of the Sacred Grove in the nave of its high chapel. Sixty years later in a poetry workshop in New Smyrna Beach, Florida, I would write an assigned poem to explain to my multi-faith new friends. Excerpts from the poem:

> Suppose he really saw the vision, God, the angel
> My church owns the story: Joseph in the grove, fourteen
> A supernatural sight of extraordinary beauty and significance …
> The boy kneeling at the elevated feet of the Father and the Son …
> While praying for a truth that had eluded others.
> A supernatural sight of extraordinary beauty and significance

And later, after a life-altering accident on the freeway and near-death experience, a realization:

> Not until today this small comet in my scalp
> The clattering of memory: the painting
> In the chapel of my childhood against the organ loft
> Joseph kneeling at the elevated feet of the Father and the Son.
> Did the artist put it in, the vision, or did I?
> The Sacred Grove: Sun streaming on the boy at prayer
> Indelible on knowing, like the features of a mother giving milk
> In the chapel of my childhood against the organ loft
> The vision.[1]

The following year I was in that ward for a missionary farewell where I'd not been for maybe thirty years. I spent the whole meeting enthralled with the painting. No boy at prayer. No Father. No Son. Only the garden. But the vision as real to me as my place at the dinner table with Mother and Father and my brothers.

Along the years I've had questions about trying to institutionalize faith, about this organizational behavior or that that seemed like sanctioning of ill will, disciplining thinkers, and discouraging publications like *Sunstone* and *Dialogue*. But this has always been my church, in it my people, of like and unlike persuasions. Even as I might struggle with seeing both sides of a question, I would be cosmically orphaned without it. Individual in believing, responding by affinity differently to different leaders, I'm thankful for various kinds of goodness to be drawn to.

In 1985 I spoke at the "Pillars of My Faith" session of Sunstone. While still believing as well as questing since, I have found that life both inside and outside the church has expanded the sense of direction I knew at that time. Out of a death experience a year after that presentation I wrote, "The pillars of my faith are still intact, but the roof has blown blessedly off the structure to reveal a whole sky full of stars." In *The Place of Knowing, A Spiritual Autobiography*, I speak of where my spiritual journey has taken me.[2] Let me explain. Those twenty-four years ago I was wife of Mel Thayne, mother of five daughters, two grandchildren, recently part of the YWMIA General Board, and only woman (for seventeen years) on the Deseret News Board of Directors. My church orientation was downtown, in the heart of the church, in intimate acquaintance with the running of it by men I esteemed around that big table in the Church Office Building at 47 East South Temple. I had weekly engagement with co-chairmen Tom Monson and Jim Faust, discussed issues with Bishop Victor Brown, Apostles Neal Maxwell, Dallin Oaks, and Jeff Holland, as well as others I respected as part of the paper—Wendell Ashton, Bill Smart, Glen Snarr, and Jim Mortimer. Banker Bob Bischoff was the token non-Mormon and I the token woman, but we were never treated as such. I felt I was there to represent those seldom represented in such a forum, the staff, the readers, and women. Despite frustrations and losing as many promptings as I won, we were friends about the business of seeing the *Deseret News* through an era of competitive and challenging readership into the age of computers and the internet that would overwhelm the print industry. Those compatriots in solving business matters have stayed friends and part of my loyalty as well as my connectedness to the church.

Such has been my association in the heart of the church. From those men and the women on the General YWMIA Board led by inimitable Florence Jacobsen and inspired by gutsy, talented, diverse, and forever friends on Mia Maid, Laurel, and Writing Committees concerned with a worldwide teaching of lessons and offering of programs. It was for one of those programs—a June Conference—that I wrote in an hour of great need words for what was to become my testimony, "Where Can I Turn for Peace?":

> Where can I turn for peace?
> Where is my solace
> When other sources cease to make me whole?
> When with a wounded heart, anger, or malice,
> I draw myself apart,
> Searching my soul?
>
> Where, when my aching grows,
> Where, when I languish,
> Where, in my need to know, where can I run?
> Where is the quiet hand to calm my anguish?
> Who, who can understand?
> He, only One.
>
> He answers privately,
> Reaches my reaching
> In my Gethsemane, Savior and Friend.
> Gentle the peace he finds for my beseeching.
> Constant he is and kind,
> Love without end.[3]

I called my music friend, Jolene Meredith. She sat at her piano, and as I read a line, she composed a line. In an hour, we had our closing song. At the time, our oldest of five daughters had suffered for three and a half years from a terrifying bout of manic depression and bulimia. Joleen was battling a familial depression herself. In 1970 the church had not addressed the possibility of either disorder. Years later, the *Church News* invited me to write about the hymn in an issue centered on a search for peace, privately and globally. The hymn would never have happened without our companionship on that Laurel committee.

This leads me to *Affection*. The eight of us "Laurels" have been eating and laughing together ever since. Pure serendipity, the affection of those dears so different from each other. Four married, four single, they brought more diversity than conformity to our so congenial efforts.

Much like my reading and writing for *Sunstone, Dialogue, and Exponent II* along with the *Improvement Era, Children's Friend, Ensign,* and *Church News,* I have grown richer through the enlightening balance I have found in them.

Those were also years of heading a dedicated writing committee of gifted men and women to prepare lessons rooting girls not only in the gospel, but in real life. We booby trapped a lesson with questions so it couldn't be just read aloud and always urged a teacher to adapt, adapt, adapt to suit her class. I also taught lessons for Relief Society, literature "out of the best books," and was intriguingly taught by resourceful others about social relations and cultural refinement as well as theology. So how can I help but be saddened as those lessons have all become theology, written by men, about men with quotes only by men yet intended for women, with admonitions not to add or subtract from what's in the manual. Still, the affection for everyone concerned lives on.

In 1985, for me the church was mostly downtown. Now, "The Church" is our ward up the street where we've lived for fifty-four years. Talk about *Affection!* About two decades ago our entire bishopric set me apart as a ward greeter. (I was often late and always chatted on my way to our "comfort zone" in the chapel.) How better to harness my wanting to stay in touch, literally and figuratively, than in hugs and handshakes with belongers as dear as my Laurel committee or friends on a board? Recently, forty of those dear Relief Society sisters from our ward gathered at our cabin as we have for years. Old, young, and in between, different from each other as the color of their hair, in a natural setting different from sitting in a classroom. Each told a line from a favorite song and we sang it to two guitars, as filled with affection for each other and the gospel that brings us together as for the thorough forest and blue sky. God's world put arms around us.

I get to give talks near and far and find the same willingness to care for and about members and nonmembers. On Tuesdays, I visit in the Temple View Room of the Salt Lake Temple with those without recommends, sometimes waiting impatiently for a marriage or sealing, some just touring. My calling is to make them feel not marginalized, but to get acquainted with their places and penchants. I've met fascinating people. About Mormonism? I wish I could introduce them to my spiritual home right up our street, still full of surprise and learning. And living life and believing.

Once a Jewish poet friend asked me why I stay Mormon. I wrote about Helen Keller in the Tabernacle in the 1930s, her outstretched hand on the back of the organ, as Alexander Schreiner played "Come, Come Ye Saints." Helen Keller cried. The little girl felt it, the seeing without seeing, the hearing without hearing, the going by feel toward something holy, something that could make her cry and could touch the heart of a little girl like the sway of wind in willows. It happens all the time, that believing. Through life as well as the Mormonism I love.

And so I live in a kind of naïveté of the spirit with allegiance, affinity, and affection holding me gently above water.

I've received forgiveness for frailties and impunity for living outside the memo world. I've voiced my contrary opinions and been mellowed by those contrary to mine.

I've found that lost causes can be as forgettable as illnesses or surgeries, not to be ignored, but dealt with expecting healing.

As Helen Keller says about her country, I say about my church—If I did not love it so much I would not wish to mend her flaws as well as accept her strengths.

Mostly, it's just plain loving what's there:

Like a grandson in an ill-fitting suit at a pulpit telling of finding his way to believing enough to head to Paraguay for two years and, like a list of fifty-four from his high school headed for New Zealand, Albania, or Tooele, to absorb a culture as well as promulgate his faith. Regardless of their eventualities, off to a spiritual maturing peculiar to a peculiar chance to grow.

It's his cousin just months before telling in touching directness how he came from skateboarding to going to North Carolina and coming to love people in the Bible Belt so unlike him, in tears giving his testimony.

It's a young father giving a name and a blessing to his baby girl to find herself in caring about others.

It's a special Primary boy reciting a poem I'd written for him for Mothers' Day, remembering every word and grinning as he finishes.

It's a Down Syndrome eighteen-year old bearing her testimony at the pulpit to a smiling congregation.

It's a string ensemble in our ward at Easter with a Jewish violist joining in.

It's a bishop giving me a blessing to get past a too-long illness, invoking Father and Mother in Heaven.

It's a forever nurse friend with blessing in her daily back rub after surgery.

It's a leader sanctioning a new idea without a memo or precedent.

It's hearing a talk at a Mormon funeral with three objects in mind: to honor the dead, to comfort the living, to contemplate the eternal. And to say it's okay to grieve as well as to believe. It's "The Plan" in action.

It's joining my uncertain voice in my dear congregation singing "Oh How Lovely Was the Morning," as others harmonize around me.

It's tearing up as our five daughters play "Love at Home" in sacrament meeting, their violins, flute, and piano as congenial as our times hiking or water skiing.

It's my husband sealing our mid-life daughter and her new husband in the Manti Temple after an agonizing divorce, surrounded by loving family and friends both inside and outside.

It's fasting in a common faith for whatever the will of the Lord for a desperately ill neighbor—and expecting peace.

It's a young elder in Hong Kong after translating sacrament meeting in Mandarin, telling me he loves our hymn—"If I weren't a missionary, I'd like a hug," me replying, "I'm not a missionary—and I could be your grandmother." Some hug!

It's help around the block and around the world offered in emergency aid to Mormons and non-Mormons alike.

I have no idea how this computer or my cell phone work, I only know that they do. In the same way, I know that God operates within law and influences my doings, just as surely, and at my choosing to connect.

Do I write as a woman? As a mother? As a wife? As a Mormon? All are inseparable as smoke and flame. I have simply to live and write by what I love.

Through allegiance, affinity, and affection, the pillars of my faith are still intact, and, yes, the roof has blown blessedly off the structure to reveal a whole sky full of stars. I wonder what the next how many years of the counseling of life might have to say about why I stay both here and then there. Negative only now and then, that wondering. I can hardly wait to see. Like a saying by Gordon B. Hinckley given me by a daughter mounted on the mantel beside where I ride my recumbent bike, so like those in my Highland Park Ward eighty years ago: "Life is to be enjoyed, not just endured." Yes, yes, yes.

Notes

1. Emma Lou Thayne, "Second Meditation: The Comet Is a Certain Light"; "Meditations on the Heavens," *Dialogue: A Journal of Mormon Thought* 20 (Summer 1987): 143–46; also in Emma Lou Thayne, *Things Happen: Poems of Survival* (Salt Lake City: Signature Books, 1991).

2. Bloomington, Indiana: iUniverse, 2011.

3. At www.lds.org/music/library/hymns/where-can-i-turn-for-peace.

Emma Lou Warner Thayne died on December 6, 2014.

It Helps Me to Become a Better Person

Ronda Roberts-Callister

A significant transition in my faith began many years ago when I was reading the Book of Abraham in the Pearl of Great Price. It had nothing to do with questions about the book's origins, but rather about Abraham being taught by the Lord. I could see no place for me as a woman within this cosmology. This raised concerns that were directly related to decisions I was wrestling with at the time. I was happily expecting my second child and finishing my master's degree, and I was preoccupied with the question of how I was going to navigate my life in the face of these two major transitions. I wanted to be a good wife and mother and yet wondered how I was going to fulfill my deep desire to continue learning and make a difference in the world while fulfilling these traditional women's callings.

As I read the scriptures, I pondered whether the tensions I was feeling could be resolved, in this life or in the eternities, especially given that the only role for women in the hereafter alluded to in LDS teachings was eternal procreation. Looking back now, I see how my experience was similar to that of many other women, especially those who did not want to be defined solely by their roles in family relationships.

These thoughts led me to want to know more about our heavenly mother. My logic was that if I knew more about her, I would have greater understanding about how women fit into the eternal scheme of things. I also hoped to answer my more important question that was too painful even to ask—how do I as a woman find a sense of value or worth within this very masculine church?

I felt especially constrained during this period because in the 1970s rhetoric from the pulpit was especially frequent and insistent in counseling mothers to stay home with their children. But President Spencer W. Kimball also counseled women to develop their talents. The dilemma for me was that my talents were not particularly home centered. I wondered, therefore, if I was expected to deny the parts of myself that could not easily be developed or expressed within the home.

As I say, in reading Abraham that day, I felt overwhelmed by the desire to know more about Mother in Heaven, hoping this would allow me to better see a path. I had begun asking questions about Mother in Heaven in 1980, the year after Sonia Johnson was excommunicated from the church in the battle over the Equal Rights Amendment. It seemed that a silence fell over women in the church following that event. As I started tentatively to ask questions, I was aware of a palpable fear of speaking about women's issues among my Mormon women. While I now know that there were LDS women willing to talk about such matters, I was not aware of any at that time.

Because I was unable to find answers or even thoughtful people to discuss my questions, over time the questions and the pain gradually receded to the proverbial shelf in my mind as I gave up my search and decided to become involved in community work satisfying my desire to make a contribution.

Six years later, when we had four young children, my husband, Mike, began medical school. Big questions were off the table as keeping up with daily life took every ounce of my energy. As a result of being unable to keep up with everything that needed doing, I became overwhelmed with guilt. Towards the end of Mike's second year of medical school, I slipped into depression caused by feelings of failure at my inability to be a good wife and mother.

Slowly, I began working my way out of depression by painstakingly learning to change the way I talked to myself and by learning to be more forgiving and accepting of my limitations. Gradually, I began feeling better and as a result felt the need to continue learning.

During this time, I attended a "Pillars of My Faith" presentation at the 1989 Sunstone symposium given by Kathleen Flake that turned out to be pivotal. As I reflected on the description of her personal story, I had a very clear impression that it was time for me to reopen my questions about our heavenly mother and about women and, their place in the church. Amazingly, it was shortly after this that I saw an advertisement for Carolyn Lynn Pearson's Salt Lake City performance of her play, *Mother Wove the Morning* (self published, 1992). It felt as though a lifeline had been thrown to me. Not only was the play fabulous, but Carol Lynn included a list of references in the program that formed the beginning of my reading. For the next year, I read every book she listed that I could track down and found others as I searched the references in those books.

It is interesting that I was not in pain at this time. The intervening years since my questions first rocked my faith had diminished the pain, and I was better able to ask questions from a relatively peaceful place. Over the next year as I read continuously, I pulled my beliefs apart and examined them; I looked around curiously at the pieces of my faith scattered about and wondered if they would ever fit back together into anything that might resemble a testimony.

As I kept reading and thinking, I began to reassemble many of the pieces, while tossing out a few completely. At this time I found the writings of Margaret Toscano and Janice Allred and the Mormon Women's Forum useful. Margaret's chapter on the temple in her book with her husband, Paul, *Strangers in Paradox: Explorations in Mormon Theology*,[1] helped me to see the temple more symbolically and therefore kept me from rejecting the temple ceremony. I still find it very sad that Margaret's and Janice's writings helped me stay in the church and yet they were not allowed to stay.

As I finished the year 1990, I put my beliefs back together again. The biggest change occurred not because I found the answers to my questions, but because I now felt responsible for my own beliefs. I became more willing to examine any issue carefully and to make my own decisions. My pain receded as I looked less to external sources for my sense of worth and well-being and more to my internal resources. That is, I began trusting myself to examine questions and to consider answers as I remained open to reexamining my beliefs with new information and insights.

At the same time, I continued actively participating in Mormonism. On the outside, I looked and acted essentially as I had before; I just thought differently. The transition in the way I thought moved me from a follower to an engaged thinker. This felt like a seismic shift.

Some years later, my husband, Mike, began having his own faith transition in which he examined a wide range of historical, doctrinal, and cultural issues.[2] Once I overcame my fear of how his faith transition might impact our marriage, we had many rich discussions. Prior to this, I had not thought about or questioned most of the issues he raised. Our discussions helped us discover significant differences as well as similarities in how we viewed these questions and refined our answers. When we discussed what we each thought, felt, or believed, I realized that many of his questions were very different from my own.

It has taken me some time to understand how better to explain my views on faith. I would like to credit a presentation my friend Dave Christian made some years ago for pointing out a useful tool for understanding the forms that faith can take. He referenced a continuum from *utility*, which includes a primary focus on usefulness, to *validity*, which includes a heavy focus on truth.[3] As Dave explained, *utility* is a practical approach that asks, "Is faith helpful?" In other words, "How well is a particular person's practice of faith promoting his or her own wellbeing? This approach is reflected in such scriptures as "By their fruits ye shall know them" (Matt. 7:20), "Ye shall know them by their fruits" (Matt. 7:16), and "Whatsoever thing persuadeth men to do good is of me; for good cometh of none save it be of me. I am the same that leadeth men to all good. ... I am the light, and the life, and the truth of the world" (Ether 4:12).

The *utility* approach is also based on the "spirit of the law." Jesus routinely rebuked the Pharisees for their legalistic rigidity in adhering to the letter of the law: When they accused him of breaking the Sabbath when his disciples plucked ears of corn, he said, "The Sabbath was made for man, and not man for the Sabbath" (Mark 2:27). Thus, the *utility* approach focuses on the consequences of faith in this world, consequences that can be evaluated here and now.

By contrast, the *validity* approach focuses predominately on determining what is true and abiding strictly by it. Using this approach, individuals must ascertain whether ideas are valid by relying on scripture, authority, prayer, revelation, and rules. With *validity*, the focus is often on the next world. For example, "Doing X will help you reach the Celestial Kingdom." When church leaders say something is either true or false, they are coming from a *validity* perspective. Most testimonies are also shared from a *validity* perspective, typically with a series of "I know" statements.

I do not know whether there is any advantage of being one side of the spectrum *(utility)* or the other *(validity)* or whether being in the middle is the most desirable, but as soon as I understood the distinction between the two, I immediately recognized that I fall on the side of *utility.* I have found over time that specific beliefs matter much less to me than an overarching framework of how I live my life. "Truth" is less important to me now than the usefulness or value I find in Mormonism in my daily life. Therefore, I tend to see my purpose in life as trying to do good in the world while working to become my best self—kinder, wiser, more compassionate, and more generous. When I consider why I stay, my primary question is, "Is the church helping me to become a better person?" As long as I continue to find value and to feel inspired to be a better person, I choose to stay.

There is a lot that I don't know. For example, I don't know with certainty whether Lehi, Sariah, and Nephi really existed, but I do know that often when I read the Book of Mormon, I feel lifted and inspired. Not always, not every chapter, but often enough that I come back again. Let me share an example: A few months ago I read King Benjamin's address: "I say unto the poor, ye who have not and yet have sufficient, that ye remain from day to day; I mean all you who deny the beggar, because ye have not; I would that ye say in your hearts that: I give not because I have not, but if I had I would give. And now, if ye say this in your hearts ye remain guiltless, otherwise ye are condemned" (Mosiah 4:24–25).

I had read these verses many times in the past and found little personal relevance. However, as I read them this time, an experience I had had twenty-five years ago came to mind. It was when I went to visit an elderly next door neighbor who had recently moved to a long-term care facility.

It was days before Christmas, and I found her discouraged and sad. She said she wanted to give something back. The Savior had blessed her life so much, she felt a desire to do something for him by serving others. As she lay in her hospital bed weeping, I tried to think of something comforting to say. I was essentially speechless. Nothing in my life up until that time helped me understand how to offer comfort to this dear neighbor, now that her physical body would not allow her to provide service to others. I left feeling that I did not have the words or the knowledge to comfort her.

But now, years later, possibly because I can now feel myself aging, this scripture from Mosiah helps me to understand how I could have comforted my neighbor by sharing this scripture with her and telling her that the Lord knew the desires of her heart and her heart was clearly in the right place. Periodic insights like this are part of why I stay.

I also deeply value the community structure created by the church that puts us together in wards by geographic location. As a result, we have greater opportunity to interact with and learn to love and care for those who may see, think, and act differently from how we do. Thich Nhat Hanh, the prominent Buddhist teacher, says, "It helps very much to have a community in which all members are sharing the same practice. In fact, it is crucial to be in a church or Sangha [a Buddhist community] in which everyone practices together. ... We need to create such communities for our own benefit" (61); and: "With all of their shortcomings [such places] are the best way to make teachings available to people" (70).[4]

I know that being part of such a community can be challenging, I also see my ward community as providing a way for me to learn and grow precisely because it encourages me to learn to understand the perspectives of others. Being part of a ward helps me become less rigid and judgmental in my perspectives because I am challenged to look beyond people's ideology and personalities and into their hearts.

In addition, the church has embedded in me the desire to serve, and it creates opportunities for service that are important to me. I value the sense of community within the LDS Church because my ward is where I have had some of my most important opportunities to serve others. For example, I once visit taught a less active sister. There was no intersection in the ways we lived our lives or the places we worked or shopped or engaged in activities. Had I not been her visiting teacher, it is highly unlikely I would ever have had any meaningful interaction with her. One day she called to tell me that her husband had had an affair with her best friend and now was leaving her. For the next year, our lives became intertwined as she reached out to me and others for moral support. She spent the next Christmas Eve with my family while her children were with their father. I sat next to her in court when she needed moral support and next to her in church as she returned to activity. I cherished this opportunity to serve at this difficult time in her life.

So I stay in the church because through personal inspiration, through reading the scriptures, through being a committed member of my own congregation, and through service to others, it helps me to become a better person.

Notes

1. Published in 1990 by Signature Books, Salt Lake City. See chap. 22, "Rending the Veil," 265–77.

2. Mike Callister, "The Forbidden Zone," Sunstone Symposium 2008; see "Planet of the Apes," www.youtube.com/watch?v=I-Rbke-gbTs.

3. *Mormon Stories Podcast*, #253: "The LDS Church and Mental Health," with Dr. David Christian, Apr. 22, 2011, at www.mormonstories.

4. *Living Buddha, Living Christ* (New York: Riverhead Books, 2007).

To Grow the Kingdom

Dan Wotherspoon

I "feel" my way through life much of the time. I love to think of myself as a smart guy, but experience after experience has shown me that my best decisions are not the ones initiated in my head but the ones that I make after carefully examining my feelings: Why was it that I reacted that way when I met this person, read this book, or had that experience? The older I've gotten, the more I've come to trust my feelings—especially the persistent ones—as data that deserve every bit as much, if not more, consideration as I construct and reconstruct my understanding of my life and the wider world, and as I decide where and how to spend my time and effort.

I bring this up at the beginning of this short reflection on "Why I Stay" actively engaged in Mormonism because the persistent feeling that I have most days I attend church meetings and engage members of my ward and the extended LDS community is one of happiness and peace. My brain definitely still kicks in regularly: *"Hey, did you notice THAT?!"* It makes sure I see every short-sighted action or closed-minded comment, every move or statement that seems motivated by fear more than love, by the letter rather than the spirit of the law. But even through all of that, somehow the feeling remains. I'm content here. I want to stay.

My earliest temple-going experiences were all about my head. What on earth is going on here? What can this symbol mean; why this action? And, of course, my ego demanded that I learn all my parts perfectly. Gotta impress those temple workers by my faultless memorization! After a while though, I learned to relax into the endowment, to put my cognitive filters in the background, and to enjoy simply being there in the temple with my fellow Latter-day Saints and seeking connection with the wider human family and life's deep purposes. The actual words spoken and actions performed became of minimal importance, far overshadowed by the feelings I felt while in that holy space.

Something similar has happened to me during the past dozen or so years of weekly church attendance. Oh sure, I am still very interested that what is said and done there employs our best gospel understandings, and I want to perform my various parts well. (And, heck, if my fellow ward members want to think of me as a "smarty," who am I to want to dissuade them?) But somehow even amidst the occasional (okay, not so occasional) bad theology and alienating rhetoric and actions that are common when regularly attending and actively watching the church as it acts on larger stages, my persistent feeling is one of affection for this my strange and quirky and wildly imperfect religious family. What the church itself and the members immediately around me do that drives me crazy is far overshadowed by feelings of love because of who they have shown me they are. Like me, they want good things for themselves, their family, their community, and their world—and though our pace is maddening at times, in our bumbling ways, we're moving in the right direction, even if sometimes our course corrections have to be preceded by backward steps.

The time in my week when I most often take the chance to examine these feelings about the church and my decision to stay engaged is during the sacrament. And this past year or so, my meditations during the sacrament service have been enlivened by a few notions that I'd like to briefly pay tribute to. The first came from a wonderful piece by Kathleen Flake in an issue of *Sunstone* magazine in which she expounds on extra elements that Latter-day Saint scripture and theology bring to sacrament worship, including the notion of the sacrament being a communal meal—a celebration of the hour in which Christ was with his disciples and their anticipation of future experiences with him.[1]

Bill Hansen also contributed a beautiful element to my sacrament meditations through his participation on a Sunstone panel session on films that have expanded his spiritual life. In that session, he reflected on two films, *Babbette's Feast* and *Pieces of April,* but he put them in the context of their being stories in which rifts are healed through the act of sharing a meal and the idea that nowhere does the spiritual meet the temporal in quite the same way as it does at a table where people break bread together. In that same session, Bill also talked about a John Dominic Crossan comment about the importance in the ancient world of "commensality" and the "commensal relationship," and how food has played such an important role in establishing and deepening relationships.[2] My recalling of this symposium session and Bill's wonderful remarks have also drawn me this year to re-watch and be deeply nourished by two films that very directly portray the sacrament as a ritual meal aimed at reconciliation. The first, *Places in the Heart*, the depression-era film in which Sally Field portrays a widow struggling to keep her land and succeeding through the aid of an unlikely group of friends, family, and strangers, ends with a scene in church in which the bread and wine are passed from congregant to congregant (including some not physically present in the meeting, such as her deceased husband and the young Black boy who killed him and who was then lynched by town members). As they partake of the emblems of Christ's sacrifice, we see them reconciling with each other as they softly speak the words "peace of God" before drinking the wine.

The other film is Richard Dutcher's powerful closing scene in *Brigham City* in which an entire LDS congregation refuses to partake of the sacrament until their bishop, who had chosen not to partake of it because he was feeling guilty about his not being able to stop certain tragic events from happening, accepts their act of solidarity and finally partakes.

Each week during the sacrament service in my ward, I often find myself looking around at my fellow ward members, most of them people whom, before I got to know them a bit I otherwise wouldn't very likely have chosen to be with, and feeling very privileged to share this sacred meal with them and experiencing how all differences or conflicts are somehow melting away.

In her article, Kathleen Flake suggests that the way Christ asks to be remembered by all who would be his disciples is through our "sharing a meal and sharing a life" with each other. I "stay" because this call is exactly one I want to answer.

As I reflected on the invitation to speak on this subject, I knew immediately that I would share something along the lines of what I have just said. But as I pondered a bit longer, it occurred to me that if

I weren't happy in my day-to-day church relationships, the only reason I'd still probably choose *not* to stay would be because I found somewhere better to go, some other tradition that contained more of what I considered truth or that was a much closer fit for my spiritual and intellectual temperament. In short, the only real reason I can think of that might ever lead me to leave Mormonism rather than simply slip into inactivity is because of my keen awareness of all the wonderful truths and gifts practiced by other religions.

Some years ago, this was indeed an issue. As a student of other faiths and thought traditions, in several cases I dove so deeply into the beauties and insights of these faiths that I was, at times, quite tempted to consider joining their ranks. I was then suffering (and still at times suffer) from what Krister Stendahl calls "holy envy," the feeling that there is something in another religious tradition that I really value and wish my tradition had, or at least that it had developed and emphasized more thoroughly.[3]

At times this envy takes on added depth of feeling to become what Stanford University religion scholar and ethicist Lee Yearly calls the emotion of "spiritual regret," the realization coupled with feeling that it's impossible to be more than one person at a time and yet still wish we could be.[4] It is the mixed experience of joy and regret at being given the life we have been given, and knowing that even though there are so many wonderful forms of human flourishing in the world, no one of us can fully experience them all.

I have been helped to transform this feeling into something less painful, even to the point where I now find it an exhilarating proposition, through my work with Charles Randall Paul at the Foundation for Interreligious Diplomacy. One of the questions that naturally comes up for theists who ponder the existence and flourishing of other religious traditions, especially non-theistic ones, is why God would design the world the way it is. And if not design it to have so many religions, at least to allow and seemingly even encourage such diversity through giving people strong spiritual confirmations about the truth and importance of their own individual traditions. If God is love, in what way is it loving to individuals or the world to order things to be this way? If there really is only one true way, wouldn't it be more loving to tell everyone, once and for all, what that way is? Surely God is powerful enough to do that!

In our musings together on this subject, Randy and I have come up with a speculative position that I find exciting. I'll share only a small portion of what we're working on, but it begins with the descriptive fact that no human being, given the limits of humanness, can possibly grasp *every* truth. Every moment we choose to pay attention to this or that truth, but it's impossible for anyone to genuinely focus on multiple, complex truths. Hence one might consider it loving of God to ask us to truly learn and inhabit only a small portion of the wondrous truths that make up all reality.

But there's also another angle on this issue, and that is to ask how it might also be important and honoring *to the different truths themselves* for God to encourage the full flourishing of many faiths. In taking our thought in this direction, I was nudged by a statement by Krista Tippett in her book, *Speaking of Faith*. Through conversing with hundreds of amazing religious people, she says:

> I began to imagine religious truth as something splintered and far-flung— for good reason, [as it was] too vast for one tradition to encompass. I saw [Christian] reformers across time as people who noticed a scattered piece of the Christian truth that the church itself was neglecting. They picked it up and loved its beauty, and saw it as necessary, and embodied its virtues. The Anglicans saw common prayer, Lutherans saw the Bible, Mennonites saw pacifism, Calvinists saw intellectual rigor, and the Quakers saw silence. And the multitudinous traditions I haven't named in that inadequate summary see nuances of those pieces of truth and other aspects altogether, all of which make the whole more vivid, more possible, in the world.

She continues: "This analogy holds as I now [go deeper into] explor[ing] the splinters of all of the world's traditions. The gentle single-mindedness of Zen complements the searching discipline of Theravada Buddhism. The exuberant spirituality of Sufism rises to meet the daily lived piety of Sunni and Shiite Islam [and so on]."[5]

From this statement to the idea of reformers seeing some piece being neglected and therefore picking it up and loving its beauty, and even seeing it as essential, and then embodying its virtues, I will take this motivation even deeper and suggest it as even being God's *will*:

and S. Burkhalter, eds., *Beyond the Classics? Essays on Religious Studies and Liberal Education* (Atlanta, Georgia: Scholars Press, 1990), 89–105.

5. Krista Tippett, *Speaking of Faith: Why Religion Matters—and How to Talk About It* (Penguin Books: 2007), 172–73.

6. B.H. Roberts, "Book of Mormon Translation," *Improvement Era* 9 (1906): 713.

Going about Doing Good

Kathleen Cattani

Mormons are indefatigable genealogists. One of the branches of particular interest in my family genealogy is my mother's maternal line. It traces her lineage back through my grandmother, Florence Orzella Marsh, my great-grandmother, Florie Green, born in England in 1884, and Florie's father, Theophilus Green, born in 1860, also in England. From there, the genealogy becomes more difficult. Theophilus Green's mother is listed as Matilda Green, born in 1841; his father is listed as "She Wouldn't Say." Thus, I am the great-great-great-granddaughter of "She Wouldn't Say."

When I first considered the question as to why I stay in Mormonism, my impulse was to echo my great-great-grandmother's response as to her paternity—"She wouldn't say." On deeper reflection, however, I began to think seriously about my reasons for staying in Mormonism and considered it an opportunity to reflect on my spiritual life, including my struggles, doubts, and questions and my hopes, faith, and life stories.

At times I have been tempted to leave the church. In 2008 when Proposition 8 passed defining marriage in California as being between one man and one woman, my husband and I were so discouraged we simply skipped church the Sunday after the election. We did not have the heart to go. That autumn had been difficult for us. We live in a ward in the San Francisco Bay Area and it felt as though we, along with my in-laws who attend the same ward, were the only members who opposed Prop 8. If other members were against it, they did not speak out about it. It was a lonely time.

When Proposition 8 passed, my husband and I asked ourselves why we were still part of an organization that we felt not only sanctioned discrimination within its ranks but took an active role in ensuring discrimination outside its own organization. But then I wondered why I was reacting so strongly to the church's position on gay marriage; I have lived with the church's restrictive position on women and the priesthood all of my life. I am also personally familiar with the church's seeming reluctance to acknowledge any family unit other than the traditional family.

I did not get married until I was forty and then married a man with two children who at the time were eight and nine. We then had a son of our own. My husband had been born and raised in the church but was inactive for most of his adult life. He re-activated when he met me and together we have been raising our three sons in the church. After each of our older boys received the Aaronic Priesthood, the ward clerk dutifully handed me their Individual Ordinance Summary. Conspicuously absent from their record was my name. I was not listed as their stepmother, nor was I even listed as the current spouse of their father. While I can appreciate that their biological mother (even though she is outspokenly anti-LDS) should be included on their record, I found it ironic that the woman who was primarily responsible for their activity in the church, not to mention their eating their vegetables, was not included. At least on all the school forms, the camp forms, and medical forms there is a place for me as an important person in their lives.

But I digress. The church's position on gay marriage felt as though it might be the proverbial straw that breaks the camel's back. My husband and I determined that if it weren't for the fact that we were raising teenagers we would stop going. We appreciated the fact that we were benefitting from the influence of good people in our lives and the lives of our children, including priesthood, seminary, and the Young Men's program, which have provided a safe haven for them.

But in reality it is not so simple. To really understand why I stay, I have to look to the past as well as to the present and the future. I realize the reasons I give today may be different from those I might give in the future as convictions and understanding often change based on experience, perspective, and time. In any event, I offer the following reflections on why I am still here.

I come from a family with a strong and abiding faith in the LDS

Church. Two of my great grandparents converted to Mormonism in Europe and came to America to practice their new faith. Another ancestor crossed the plains. My parents met in the 1950s LDS version of the young adult program in Southern California. My mother was president of the Golden Gleaners and my father was the president of the Master M-Men. After marrying in the St. George, Utah, temple, they graduated from Brigham Young University and raised their five children in the church. All five of us graduated from BYU, and four of us served proselytizing missions. My father served in a bishopric when I was a child growing up in Arizona and my mother was the stake girl's camp director for thirteen years.

In conjunction with their faith and activity, my parents also subscribed to *Dialogue: A Journal of Mormon Thought* and *Sunstone*. In the 1970s my mother worked because she wanted to, not because she had to, and she was vocal in her support of the Equal Rights Amendment. The loneliness my husband and I felt during the church's campaign in favor of Prop 8 brought to mind what my mother must have felt during the church's campaign against ratification of the ERA.

I have conscientiously attended church for most of my life, and I have served in many callings, including my current calling in the children's Primary. I have worked hard to be a standard Mormon, but, in all honesty, I don't always feel like one. For most of my adult life, I have felt more on the fringe of the church or, to use a Sunstone term, on the borderland.

As I have gotten older and faced more challenges and the realities in life, I find that I "know" a lot less now than I used to. I no longer have the same clarity of conviction, of "knowing" that something is true, as I did when I returned from my mission. I am not wired like those who prefer the moral clarity of a black-and-white world; somehow I see greater shades of gray with each passing year.

So why do I stay?

Several years ago I was asked to speak in a stake conference on the subject of reaffirming a testimony. The member of the stake presidency who asked me to speak was someone I had been working with in the stake primary and someone I held in high regard. In declining the opportunity, I explained that I struggle a lot with my "testimony" and couldn't say that "I know the church is true" in the sense that most people do who utter those words. This fine man replied that he understood, adding,

> Most of us who are at all self-aware experience a hunger for things spiritual. Our search can be endless and range over the universe of avenues of truth and enlightenment. In the final analysis, however, those of us who have felt the spirit and have had spiritual confirmations like those I have heard you describe from your mission, will only find joy and satisfaction when we come home—and come to terms with the emotional/spiritual experiences we have come to know at earlier stages of life.

I stay because my spiritual awakenings are rooted in the Mormon community. My identity and my world view are inextricably Mormon. Fundamentally I see myself as a child of God. While I may not have the clear and certain perspective of who God is as I did as a child, I believe in a personal, loving God who cares about me.

I stay because my parents stayed. Service was important to them and they modeled how a member could be active and involved, yet thoughtful and accepting of doubts, questions, and disbelief. I remember as a teenager having a discomforting feeling after reading an article about Joseph Smith and one of his controversial practices or teachings. Although I don't remember the specific concern, I do remember questioning my dad about it. He reassuringly reminded me that Joseph was a man as well as a prophet.

I stay because of the community that I enjoy among my fellow saints. In the book of Acts we are told that Jesus "went about doing good" (10:38). The same may be said for many of the Mormons whom I grew up with, as well as many I have met in my adult life—they have gone about doing good and my family, and I have been the beneficiary of that goodness.

When I was in college, my mother was diagnosed with a brain tumor. Complications following surgery left her partially paralyzed. In the months following her surgery, the members of our small town ward in California showed a tremendous amount of caring, love, and support. They brought food, routinely visited, and fasted and prayed for us.

Nine months later my father was diagnosed with a malignant brain tumor. After radiation treatment and a period of remission, the cancer returned. In the last months of his life, we were fortunate to be able to care for him at home. One day, we had a surprise visit from the two men my father had served with in the bishopric in Arizona more than a dozen years previously. They showed up on our California doorstep unannounced to spend the day reminiscing, sharing stories and laughing with my father. It is a visit that I will never forget.

During the last month of my father's life, the men from his high priests' quorum took turns staying with him at night so that we could sleep. One of these brothers was with my father when he died early one morning. The members of our ward brought to life the words in Mosiah about those who are willing to bear one another's burdens and to mourn with those that mourn, and comfort those that stand in need of comfort (18:8–10).

I am aware that there are many communities of faith that provide the kind of support my family experienced during these difficult times. My Baptist and Catholic friends speak fondly of the communities they grew up in. Garrison Keillor's stories of the Lutherans who live in Lake Wobegon are not unlike some of my experiences in the Mormon community. That being said, Mormonism is my community and where I belong.

Another reason I stay is because the church provides an incredible forum for service, personal growth, and self-actualization. When I was a missionary in Lima, Peru, about mid-way through my mission, I was assigned to an area in the northern part of the country that had been devastated by floods the year before. The people were poor, and children ran barefoot and half-naked around open sewers. I was feeling emotionally drained from being surrounded by so much poverty and from trying to help people who did not seem to really want our help. I sometimes wondered what kind of a futile endeavor I was engaged in and whether it was really worth the struggle. When I expressed these feelings to my mission president, he acknowledged that it was hard and quoted Joseph Smith: "A religion that does not require the sacrifice of all things never has power sufficient to produce the faith necessary unto life and salvation."[1]

So I stay for the same reason that sometimes makes me want to leave—the church requires sacrifice. However, it is those very sacrifices that have helped me to grow in ways I never could have imagined. It is the sacrifice of my time in various callings that has provided me with some of the closest friendships and relationships that I have ever had.

Finally, I stay because Mormonism offers a robust, empowering theology that inspires and challenges me. For example, I like the idea that we existed as intelligences, independent of God, before we became spiritual offspring of God. I like the idea that we are spiritual offspring of God, that we lived before we came to Earth, that we are here to learn and progress, and that we will continue to progress even after our sojourn on earth ends. I am not that interested in becoming a god or a queen or a priestess, but I love the idea that I can keep learning and progressing in the next life and that I can continue my relationships with family and friends beyond this mortal life.

Mormonism—with its many doctrines and expectations—often comes across as an all or nothing proposition. The lofty ideals and grand expectations can be overwhelming, angst-inducing, and identity-erasing. While I love many aspects of our rich theology, I have found that the "whole cloth" approach doesn't work for me. There are doctrines and teachings that mean less to me now than they did at some earlier point in my life.

In her memoir, *Eat Pray Love,* Elizabeth Gilbert quotes a "dear friend" as saying, "You don't want to go cherry-picking a religion," to which she responds, "[This] is a sentiment I completely respect except for the fact that I totally disagree." She then goes on to say, "I think you have every right to cherry-pick when it comes to moving your spirit and finding peace in God. I think you are free to search for any metaphor whatsoever which will take you across the worldly divide whenever you need to be transported or comforted. It's nothing to be embarrassed about. It's the history of mankind's search for holiness. …You take whatever works from wherever you can find it, and you keep moving toward the light."[2]

I find it works for me to cherry-pick the doctrines and teachings that resonate for me and set aside the ones that don't. As I think about my life as a Mormon and my own spiritual journey, I recognize that my understanding and interpretation of parables, stories, doctrines, even my own life stories have changed and will continue to change over time as new experiences change me. Robert Frost once wrote:

> For, dear me, why abandon a belief
> Merely because it ceases to be true.

Cling to it long enough, and not a doubt
It will turn true again, for so it goes.[3]

Whether or not I believe everything the church teaches or always see things through the same lenses as my fellow Mormons, it does not change my appreciation for my connection to this community or my commitment to principles grounded in the teachings of Christ. I am glad to be a part of a community that values love, free agency, faith, forgiveness, grace, redemption, service, and gratitude. I am grateful to associate with others who strive to be honest and true and who go about doing good.

Notes

1. Joseph Smith Jr., *Lectures on Faith*, 6:7, at www.eom.byu.edu/index.php/Lectures_on_Faith.

2. Elizabeth Gilbert, *Eat, Pray, Love: One Woman's Search for Everything* (New York: Penguin Group, 2006), 207–08.

3. Robert Frost, "The Black Cottage," in *The Complete Poems of Robert Frost* (New York: Henry Holt and Co., 1969), 77.

My Center of Gravity

Curt Bench

To write about why I stay in the church suggests that I might consider leaving, which I've never actually contemplated. Sometimes I've wondered if I should take a short break, but, alas, I'm just too busy being active to take any time off. Even though I've never really considered leaving, I have friends and associates who have, and this has given me an opportunity to consider their reasons for doing so, as well as my own reasons for staying.

Although I understand why some separate from the church, I am saddened by their leaving. I feel we are diminished as a church and people by their doing so, especially when in some cases I believe their leaving could have been avoided if we had done a better job of addressing their legitimate concerns—and if those who have such concerns looked into them more deeply.

There are many reasons why *I* stay. I am certainly not the first to say that one of the reasons is because I come from a long line of Mormons—most faithful, some less so. My LDS heritage goes back at least five generations and includes some who were in the thick of things in the early church, including a couple of real-life Danites. These stalwarts sacrificed much to live the restored gospel and serve the church. I honor them and feel a deep sense of kinship and loyalty toward them and the church they loved. I feel Mormonism down to my very bones. It's hard for me to imagine being any other place—except when I find myself enduring some especially boring or annoying meetings; then I can easily do so!

I grew up in a devout LDS home in Southern California and have done most of the usual things expected of a young male Latter-day Saint: seminary, mission, temple marriage, a variety of callings, including my favorite—Gospel Doctrine teacher. Without pushing the envelope too much, my goal as a teacher is to have those in my class walk away feeling they have learned at least one new thing or are now thinking about something in a way they haven't before. If they do, perhaps I have succeeded in some small way.

Mormonism is the only life I know. I see life through Mormon eyes. The simple yet profound teachings of the gospel of Christ as taught in the church ring true and speak to my soul. We are all brothers and sisters, offspring of God, who are taught to love, forgive, and treat others as we want to be treated. We are to care for the poor and needy and give of our substance and time. We should "be willing to bear one another's burdens, that they may be light," "to mourn with those that mourn," and "to comfort those that stand in need of comfort" (Mosiah 18:9).

Over a lifetime I have had some powerful experiences I call "random acts of inspiration" that have fortified my faith because I cannot explain them in any other way than spiritually. In addition, I have had meaningful and touching experiences with fellow Saints that have developed into lifetime bonds and friendships.

Although I see life through Mormon eyes, I do not wear rose-colored glasses. I have studied LDS Church history and doctrine all my adult life and am under no illusion that ours is a perfect church or that we have flawless leaders or members. I'm aware of most arguments of the critics and have spent considerable time pondering and weighing them. I realize our history is filled with evidence of the failings, errors, and weaknesses of its people, leaders included, which should be expected, but can be a stumbling block for some.

In an inspiring and hope-filled general conference talk in 2013, Dieter F. Uchtdorf, at the time the second counselor in the First Presidency, said:

> There have been times when members or leaders in the Church have simply made mistakes. There may have been things said or done that were not in harmony with our values, principles, or doctrine.
>
> I suppose the Church would be perfect only if it were run by perfect beings. God is perfect, and his doctrine is pure. But He works through us—His imperfect children—and imperfect people make mistakes.[1]

For nearly fifty years, I have been in the business of Mormon book-selling, the past thirty-four years as owner of Benchmark Books, which specializes in rare, used, and collectible LDS items. One can't work in a bookstore such as ours and not be exposed to counter facts and arguments, while also observing and feeling the pain of those who, troubled by difficult questions and issues, often find no answers, or resort to bad ones, with no resolution. Over the years many have called or come to our store feeling hurt, confused, or angry. As they have studied church history and then asked searching questions, they have been cautioned, rebuffed, or even ostracized by leaders and fellow members.

I have empathy for these individuals because I have had some of the same experiences. Although I have never been censured or ostracized for questioning, at times I have certainly felt the disapproval of those who think it is wrong to question or doubt. I'm grateful for a leader who assures us that questioning is not wrong. In the same conference address, Elder Uchtdorf also said:

> Some might ask, "But what about my doubts?" It's natural to have questions—the acorn of honest inquiry has often sprouted and matured into a great oak of understanding. There are few members of the Church who, at one time or another, have not wrestled with serious or sensitive questions. One of the purposes of the Church is to nurture and cultivate the seed of faith—even in the sometimes sandy soil of doubt and uncertainty. Faith is to hope for things which are not seen but which are true.[2]

I find great comfort in the exchange between Jesus and the man who brought to him his son to be healed: "Jesus said to him, If thou canst believe, all things are possible to him that believeth. And straightway the father of the child cried out, and said with tears, Lord, I believe; help thou mine unbelief" (Mark 9:23–24).

Herman Hesse affirms the coexistence of these two elements: "Faith and doubt go hand in hand; they are complementaries. One who never doubts will never truly believe."[3] Expressing my sentiments, Frederick Buechner observed succinctly that, "if there's no room for doubt, there is no room for me."[4] Citing Flannery O'Connor, who said, "I think there is no suffering greater than what is caused by the doubts of those who want to believe," LDS authors Terryl and Fiona Givens write: "Not once, but twice, the Lord prefaced His commandment that we strengthen each other with this explanation: 'As all have not faith.' He thus acknowledged that even among His modern disciples, there would be—and must be—room for those who live in doubt."[5]

I do not share some church members' need for certitude. Alma taught that faith "is not to have a perfect knowledge of things." For some reason in the church today, it seems unacceptable to say "I believe" or "I feel" something is true. Unless we "know" whatever it is "without a doubt" or "beyond a shadow of a doubt," it is implied that we are spiritually or morally lacking. Over the years, I have become more content with "believing" or even "hoping" than with "knowing." The Givenses write further that "the call to faith is a summons to engage the heart, to attune it to resonate in sympathy with principles and values and ideals that we devoutly hope are true, and that we have reasonable but not certain grounds for believing to be true. And that what we choose to embrace, to be responsive to, is the purest reflection of what we love."[6]

I am a "big tent" Mormon, feeling there is room inside for all. I subscribe to Paul's metaphor of the church as a body in which every part is necessary and valued—all honored together (1 Cor. 12).

There is something wonderful about arguing points of doctrine or history with a very conservative, Church Education System teacher on Sunday, and then on Tuesday be working side-by-side with him helping to shingle the roof of a fellow member. Our common bond as fellow Saints makes our differences seem less important and what we have in common paramount.

I look at the church as I do family (both of which can sometimes be dysfunctional): I don't always *like* my family members, but I always *love* them. I don't like everything about the church, but I love the church and its members.

There are current members and leaders of the church who inspire and motivate me by their devotion to the life of the mind while also embracing a powerful spirituality. However, not wanting to embarrass them, I will cite only examples of some departed but equally brave individuals from our history who inspire in me a deep loyalty and a desire to stay through thick and thin.

In 1857, Levi Savage spoke out against the Willie Handcart Company's leaving Iowa, warning that suffering, sickness, and death would be the result. His was the sole voice among the leaders to say so, and he was severely rebuked. His warnings proved to be accurate, if not prophetic, because over 200 handcart pioneers in the Willie and Martin companies died of starvation, exhaustion, and illness, and many of the survivors suffered greatly. Nevertheless, without bitterness or complaint, Savage had made the arduous journey with his fellow saints and demonstrated his deeply felt loyalty and compassion by working tirelessly to assist them and alleviate the suffering he had foreseen.

Against all odds, southern Utah historian and homemaker Juanita Brooks wrote a groundbreaking, courageous, and explosive book about the darkest event in Mormon history, the Mountain Meadows Massacre. Brooks was praised by many, but she was also sharply criticized, even ostracized, by some Latter-day Saints, including some leaders, who felt she had betrayed her church and people. Though stung by the criticism, she remained a loyal and dedicated Latter-day Saint and continued to write for many years. In 1978, the Mormon History Association presented Juanita Brooks with a special award for her lifetime of research and writing about the Mormon past.

Hugh B. Brown, a liberal, open-minded, and generous-hearted apostle and counselor to church president David O. McKay, stated in 1969, "We are not so much concerned with whether your thoughts are orthodox or heterodox as we are that you shall have thoughts."[7]

Lowell Bennion was an inspiring and courageous LDS Institute teacher and humanitarian who was seen by some members and leaders as too liberal. When asked why we should attend worship services even "when the experience is too often unsatisfying," Bennion replied, "To serve and to bless, to be served and blessed."[8]

Richard D. Poll was a professor of history known to many as the author of the essay, "What the Church Means to People Like Me." In this essay he coined the term "Liahona Saint," which has helped me to define my place in the church as one who "is preoccupied with questions and skeptical of answers, finding in the gospel—as he or she understands it—answers to enough important questions so as to function purposefully without answers to the rest."[9]

Marion D. Hanks, a longtime LDS Church general authority, always spoke his mind, sometimes to his detriment. He counseled literally thousands of church members who questioned their faith or commitment to the church by telling them to "stay inside and lift."[10]

I stand in awe of these individuals and gladly try to follow in their footsteps. They stayed and did much of the heavy lifting. One of the reasons I stay is because of the examples they set. They valued the life of the mind and independence of thought and yet understood the importance of recognizing our need for cultivating the life of the spirit. I share those values of all these good saints. Their courageous, faithful discipleship has shown me there is room in this church for someone like me.

Some wonder if the church is becoming more open or less open and progressive. I tend to be optimistic. Beginning with the "Camelot" years under Leonard Arrington and the "New Mormon History," we have seen candid and balanced scholarship flourish. Efforts such as the Joseph Smith Papers Project, the publication of *Massacre at Mountain Meadows* (by historians employed by the church), and many independent books and articles have made a huge contribution in the exploration of our history.

In 1978 we saw the official termination of a century-old policy that had prohibited the holding of priesthood by Black men and the admission to the temple by Black men and women, and in December 2013 some of the questionable teachings that sustained that practice were disavowed in the church's online Gospel Topics Essays series. We have seen a softening in the church's stance toward the LGBTQ community, which is especially evident in the church's revised website, www.churchofjesuschrist.org/topics/gay "Same Sex Attraction," and in the updated *General Handbook: Serving in The Church of Jesus Christ of Latter-day Saints* (see 38.6.12 "Same-Sex Attraction and Same-Sex Behavior").

There has been more conversation lately about women in the church than there has been for many years, and I believe there is more to come. Since the age requirement for female missionaries was lowered to nineteen, the number of sisters in the mission field has increased significantly. Another welcome change is the addition of sister trainer missionaries. There has also been additional visibility of women general officers including the placement of photographs of the female auxiliary presidencies in the LDS Conference Center and in the conference issue of the *Ensign*. Women, young women, and girls eight and older now meet together annually in October in the general women's session of general conference, while the priesthood session is held annually during the April conference.

Other significant changes include allowing women and children who hold temple recommends to act as witnesses for baptisms, both in and out of the temple. In addition, the 2020 *General Handbook* states that "God's priesthood power flows to all members of the Church—female and male—as they keep the covenants they have made with Him. Members make these covenants as they receive priesthood ordinances. … All Church members who keep their covenants—women, men, and children—are blessed with God's priesthood power in their homes to strengthen themselves and their families."[11]

Largely as a result of the work done within the Joseph Smith Papers Project, numerous adjustments and corrections were made to the standard works in 2013, especially in the headings to the sections and the two Official Declarations in the Doctrine and Covenants. Valuable historical context was added to clarify the dates and circumstances of the revelations as well as to the background of the declarations. In addition, the church has posted on its website several essays dealing with troubling and sensitive issues from our history such as the First Vision, polygamy, race and priesthood, DNA and the Book of Mormon, and origins of the Book of Abraham. These "Gospel Topics" do not purport to answer all the questions raised and will undoubtedly leave some dissatisfied and wanting more, but they represent progress as the church tries to forthrightly discuss issues that have troubled many for years. I hope this openness and a willingness on the part of church leaders to deal with the "hard questions" will continue apace.

Compared to where we were a generation ago, when viewed in their entirety, these changes are dramatic. They encourage me. I believe they are steps forward, albeit, perhaps, small steps. I would rather that we take bolder steps and lead instead of follow. I would also prefer we be fed meat in our curriculum instead of so much milk (often skim, at that). But I have a growing hope. We have much room for improvement, and we are making progress. The door has opened slightly and I long for the day when it is wide open.

Not long ago, one of our daughters who has difficulty believing some of our basic premises and doctrines told my wife and me about her disaffection with Mormonism and her decision to no longer be active in the church. She was disturbed by what she perceived as the hypocrisy and pettiness of some church leaders and members and with some of the negative ways women, Blacks, and gays have been treated in the church over the years.

I candidly asked my daughter if she honestly thought she had come up with questions or encountered problems in Mormonism that my wife and I had not faced or thought about. She admitted she hadn't. Then I told her that while I respected her decision and that it did not change our relationship or love in the slightest, I wished she had stayed in longer, studied, thought, and even struggled more before making her decision to leave. It takes a lot of time, patience, and experience, usually over a lifetime, to exercise the informed judgment with which to decide matters of the soul—as has certainly been the case with me. I told her then, as I have told others, I consciously choose to be Mormon, as an adult, not a child, with my eyes wide open. I agree with a friend's observation that "faith is a decision."

I have come to the conclusion that there are very few things we can know with certainty. While some live in a black and white world, I see many shades of gray. I have learned to live with ambiguity. I am content to try to exercise faith, as weak as it may be, where there is no knowledge.

Mormonism gives me a center of gravity; it is pulling constantly at me, keeping me in its orbit. I feel a kinship with and a love for my fellow Saints that run deep and true within me. Since I cannot imagine going through life without them, I don't imagine I ever will.

Notes

1. Dieter F. Uchtdorf, "Come, Join With Us," *Ensign,* Nov. 2013.

2. Ibid.

3. Hermann Hesse, *Reflections* (New York: Farrar Straus & Giroux, 1974), 291.

4. From Frederick Buechner, *The Alphabet of Grace* (New York: Harper One, 1989), 47.

5. Terryl Givens and Fiona Givens, *The Crucible of Doubt: Reflections on the Quest for Faith* (Salt Lake City: Deseret Book Co., 2014), 143.

6. Terryl Givens and Fiona Givens, *The God Who Weeps: How Mormonism Makes Sense of Life* (Salt Lake City: Deseret Book Co., 2012), 4.

7. Hugh B. Brown, "An Eternal Quest-Freedom of the Mind," in *Speeches of the Year* (Provo, Utah: Brigham Young University Press, 1969). This particular sentence appears only in the published version.

8. Molly Bennion, "I Stay to Serve and Be Served," in Robert A. Rees, ed., *Why I Stay: The Challenges of Discipleship for Contemporary Mormons* (Salt Lake City: Signature Books, 2011), 154.

9. Richard D. Poll, "What the Church Means to People Like Me," *Dialogue: A Journal of Mormon Thought* 2 (Winter 1967): 107–17.

10. Personal conversations with one of Marion D. Hanks's children.

11. *General Handbook: Serving in The Church of Jesus Christ of Latter-day Saints* (Salt Lake City: The Church of Jesus Christ of Latter-day Saints, 2020, online), 3.5, 3.6.

Within the Church, I Practice
Filling My Broken Heart with Love

Jody England Hansen

In the movie *Cowboys and Aliens* (2011), the clergyman Meacham says, "You can't expect God to do everything. You've got to earn his presence, recognize it, and act on it."

I am what they call a DNA Mormon. For some, this may stand at times for "Does Not Attend," but mostly, for me, it means that Mormonism seems integral to every cell of my body. That is due, no doubt, to my genetic, cultural, and spiritual heritage, but essentially it is due to my conscious choice to make it so. In other words, I have chosen to be and to stay Mormon.

I have come to realize that my decision is related to the fact that I am selfish and lazy. I want to be a certain kind of person, and I am too selfish and lazy to be that kind of person without help, structure, and a community that will see me as, and ask me to be, what I have promised (to God, myself, and others) to be. I stay because, when I fail to be what I want to be, they will be there to help me. It takes practice to learn how to love, to receive love, to forgive and repent, to do justly, love mercy, and walk humbly with God. That is the kind of person I want to be. Those are the kinds of people I want to be with.

I recognize that the LDS Church has its share of proud, hypocritical, intolerant people, including me, who make a lot of mistakes and frequently fail. But if I wanted to avoid interacting with such people I would have to stay away from any organization, any relationship, including members of my own family—and I would have to find a way to get away from myself. Being hypocritical, failing, proud, and intolerant is a human condition, not exclusively Mormon.

When I am not living the gospel, it seems that people are more hypocritical and intolerant. I have less patience, am suspicious, lose sleep worrying about the awful things people do, have less desire to go beyond first impressions, and am very sure that I am right about everything. Then I am not fun to be around, which means that at such times I am very lonely. When I am willing to serve and worship with people who are human, no matter how different they are from me, I get to see how powerful and life-changing love, forgiveness, and repentance can be. For example, in my ward I serve with a sister who belongs to the Tea Party, which is about as far from my political position as I can imagine. But she is the first to show up when someone is in need, never gossips, is not judgmental, and expresses love to and prayers on behalf of my loved ones and me without condition or qualification.

Recently at a planning meeting, she read a letter sent by the First Presidency encouraging members to think carefully before making judgments about the millions of illegal immigrants in our country, asking that we see all as children of God. I could tell that was she was having difficulty reconciling her political views with the counsel of the brethren. Nevertheless, she paused at the end of the letter, and said, "Well, I obviously need to pray and seek guidance about this." In that moment, I saw her heart open. I would much rather be present for such a moment than to be righteously yelling at her from opposites sides of a rally while holding a picket sign.

I acknowledge that it is hard when fellow members express views that I consider intolerant or hold opinions that have more to do with cultural tradition than with loving others as Christ loves us. But I would rather have fellowship with such people in a context in which we learn together how to live the gospel better, because there is a great possibility that, in doing so, we can change one another's hearts. It is in practicing the gospel in our daily lives that we learn how to be like Christ.

Friends ask how I can sustain leaders who are flawed or who make serious errors. I worked in the LDS Church History Department when some of the Mark Hofmann forgeries were causing controversy. I learned that even some of the most authentic-looking documents can be forgeries and thus fool almost anyone, including prophets and apostles, which means that, like all of us, they are subject to mistakes and failures. In the face of that realization, my question is, "What can I learn from their works and words?" I do not rely on the words of people who have an obvious agenda and are not interested in historical or scientific accuracy. Jon Krakauer and others like him, whose agenda is to write popular best sellers, can call their books non-fiction, but the reliability and accuracy of their sources are sometimes lacking. People like Glenn Beck and Bill Maher claim to be truthful commentators, but they make their living foremost by being entertainers. Relying on them for information about the church or church leaders makes as much sense as relying on multiple-forwarded emails written mostly in caps with many exclamation marks for accurate information about President Obama or President Trump.

I may never know all of the real truth about Joseph Smith in this life, but I do know he received revelations that help me see divinity functioning as Heavenly Parents, dynamic in their relationship with us, aware and loving us beyond our comprehension, whose greatest desire is to help us become like them and progress forever. Because of what was revealed to Joseph Smith, I understand that there are forces stronger than loss or death; that not only am I not to follow blindly, but I am responsible for seeking my own witness and revelation for my life; that God responds when we ask and show we are truly ready to hear the message; that our choices are more powerful than our circumstances; and that God will always honor our agency. All of this is something I want to be a part of.

By staying, I have been able to witness important changes. Hearing the revelation on the priesthood and temple in 1978 was powerful not only because of its subject, but also because we as a family had prayed for it for years. I saw people willing to change because of that. If I want to see more revelations, I need to be willing to be among those asking and preparing for them. By staying, I am able to see that the overall message of general conference is not the short disheartening clip on national news, but rather the many talks about love, tolerance, acceptance, looking for ways to trust and not be driven by fear.

I stay because of the temple. Each time I go, I take on someone's name, and, for a short while, I become them. Their concerns are mine, and I think mine can become theirs. I experience at-one-ment with those who live throughout time and distance, and I learn to love, through them, all people as my brothers and sisters. I also think it is possible for them to be aware of my concerns, and my loved ones have someone else who is aware of them, who reaches out to them from beyond the veil. I am also asked never to hold onto harsh feelings toward anyone, since, at any moment, it could impede my connection to God. The requirements to enter the temple become minor compared to what this brings to my life.

In the temple, I am reminded that the story of Adam and Eve is about my life. The bronze doors at St. Mary's Cathedral in Hildesheim, Germany, depict the last moments in the garden. God is there pointing an accusatory finger at Adam, who is covering himself with one hand and pointing a finger with his other hand at Eve. She is covering herself with one hand and pointing her finger at the serpent. It is a great visual depiction of humanity, our inclination to hide our shame over our actions while blaming someone else for them.

It is so tempting to want to return to the garden. No work, no pain, no responsibilities, everything handed to you. But the gospel teaches me that we are meant to take that step to leave and choose growth, progression, knowledge, and, with it, deep pain and great joy, sorrow and love, forgiveness and repentance—paradox in fulfilling our divine nature. In other words, I am asked to repent and stop being ashamed, to grow up and be responsible for my choices. The gospel covenants that begin at baptism and continue throughout life ask me to be responsible for a Christ-like life and provide me the structure that makes it possible. They ask me to have a vulnerable heart that I can allow to be broken when I see that Christ loves me enough to experience all pain possible so that I will never carry a burden alone. On my own, I tend to doubt, fear, judge, and get defensive. Within the church, I practice filling my broken heart with love.

I stay because of how I experience life. When I pray aloud, morning and night, I learn to be in constant dialogue with powers beyond my own. I learn to listen for anything, even when it might not be what I want or expect to hear, and I have been able to receive comfort, strength, and guidance in more ways than I could have imagined. And in those moments when I feel overwhelmed with worry, fear, and confusion, and there is no specific answer, there is an overwhelming experience of love, for me and for those I care about.

I stay because of the Book of Mormon. My dad taught that great books are made for the second reading. The Book of Mormon is made for the tenth, or twentieth, or thirtieth reading. When I read the Book of Mormon every day, sometimes one verse, sometimes 120 pages, I find an amazing tool for life, unlike anything else. Enos, who hungered to know even as he hungered for breath, prayed all night and experienced redemption. His words, "Lord, how is it done?" touch me. I too want to know how it is done, and am willing to allow the answer of the Atonement to lead me, like Enos, to love and care for my family, my friends, all people, and especially my enemies. That is a miracle.

I read about the father of King Limhi, who listens to his enemy teach him about a loving, merciful God. He prays to this God with such desire, he says, "I will give away all my sins to know thee." And I think of how fiercely I tend to hang on to my sins, my addictions, my pride about being right, my laziness and selfishness, at the cost of knowing God. I am inspired to give it up, for that priceless pearl.

I read in Mormon 9:31, "Condemn me not because of mine imperfection, neither my father, because of his imperfection, neither them who have written before him; but rather give thanks unto God that he hath made manifest unto you our imperfections, that ye may learn to be more wise than we have been." This reminds me that we all are here, on whatever path we choose, trying to find our way home. I can waste my energy dwelling on the mistakes of others, blaming them for obstacles in my way. Or I can look to each life around me as a contribution to my journey and see that there is always something for me to learn and be grateful for the lesson.

Staying in the church lets me learn much from imperfections. I would not want to open myself to judgment, especially by judging those who, however imperfectly, have devoted their lives to helping me find my way home. This is not a church where service wins anyone a vacation home in Hawaii. You couldn't pay me enough to do my church job. I only do it out of love—for love.

Third Nephi speaks about the terrible storms and destruction that happened at the beginning of the thirty-fourth year after the prediction of Christ's birth. In the darkness the people hear the voice of Christ witness his mission and invite them to come to him. In the next chapter it speaks about how at the end of that year, as they gathered at the temple, the voice of God introduced Christ and he appeared to them. I think of what they did during that year. What they needed to do to prepare, so they could open their ears and hear, open their eyes and see, open their hearts and feel. Whatever was needed, they were given the time so they were in the place where they could receive Christ. I think of the many times I have turned away from God, and yet his invitation is always there, his voice continues to beckon me. Christ will give me the time I need to prepare to see and hear him.

By saying the kingdom of God is within us, I think one of the most comforting and frightening teachings of Christ is that the worst hell we can imagine is the one of our own creating, and that heaven is also of our own creating. I remember hearing in Sunday school, from the time I was a child, that so much of the restoration gospel is about relationships, and how our associations last beyond death. I don't remember learning to be afraid of death or to worry about heaven or hell. In the next life, we will be with those who are like us. Not necessarily those we admire, but those who are like us, whom we relate to. However we create ourselves, now and forever, that is how and where we will be. I seek to know God as a being of unconditional love, and practice what I learn so I can be with unconditional love. I want to be with my husband, Michael, who is loving, faithful, kind, teachable, fun, strong, and willing to make and keep promises. I see him become all of that as he practices being the person he promises to be.

The person I miss the most now is my father. I want to be able to be with him after this life, and be close to him now. He is my mentor and example for living the gospel of Christ. For him, the best means to practice this was activity in the church. Each time I have sensed his presence since his death, or heard his voice when I needed it most, it is one that continues to learn, and sensing his influence makes me more willing to trust in the promises of covenants.

I stay because of the peace and comfort that comes when I don't know how I can keep going. Almost two years ago, Michael was in a serious bicycle accident. After getting calls from those who witnessed the accident and the EMTs telling me which hospital to meet them at, I hurried to the ER, calling family members and our bishop. I asked my daughter to call others and get his name on the temple rolls. I could feel the influence of others' prayers almost immediately, and I remembered how Dad would tell me, in those last months of his life, that he could feel the prayers of others bringing him strength and comfort.

When I saw Mike in the ER, he was strapped to a board, his head and neck immobilized. He was not himself, did not seem to be able to make connections with what was happening. The ER doctor told me there was severe head trauma and probably permanent damage. I became more alarmed as I kept talking with Michael, trying to see some sign of his normalcy, which was not there. I tried not to let terror overwhelm me. Then the words came to me. "Fear not, I am with you. Be not afraid, for I am thy God and will give thee aid. I'll strengthen thee, help thee, and cause thee to stand. Upheld by my righteous, omnipotent hand." A few moments later, our bishop was there with his son. He gave Mike a blessing. After he left, I continued to plead for healing powers to move through my hands into Mike. I knew that somehow, we would be able to endure this.

Just as I had experienced sacred moments that helped me endure the loss of my father, this was a moment when I knew there were powers stronger than death and loss, and I trusted in them. Within moments after the blessing was over, Mike seemed to return to himself. Soon the doctor's concern changed to surprise, then shifted to focus on the multiple broken bones and bruised lung. Mike has never regained memory of those two hours, and the physical recovery was difficult, but there have been no other signs of a brain injury.

I have not always seen blessings and prayers answered the way I want, nor when I hope. But I am able to see that I am heard, and known, even if the help comes not in a miraculous physical healing but in strength to endure and peace in times of great loss or heartbreak.

No matter what I do, I can't control the difficulties that may happen at any moment. What I can control is my willingness to see that I do not need to be on my own, that miracles may come when we are willing to let them, especially when they may be different from what we may have chosen. Left to my own devices, I quickly become arrogant and build barriers to anything unknown, different, or out of my control.

I stay for the practice that turns me away from that arrogance and toward the strength, peace, and love that are beyond all understanding.

Why I Stay

Alan D. Eastman

I am a scientist by training, occupation, and nature. You need to know that one of the chief characteristics of scientists is having the curiosity of a hyperactive five-year-old. I just like to know something about everything, and the more the better. Like many five-year-olds, besides the curiosity, I'm a collector. For example, I have two jackets covered with little cloth patches showing places I've been, plus a drawerful of patches that haven't yet found a home. I also collect aphorisms. One that is particularly relevant to the distribution of personalities at Sunstone relates to scientists' tendency to specialize and liberal-arts types' drive to expand their conclusions to cover more intellectual ground. It goes: *Scientists learn more and more about less and less until finally they know everything about nothing. Philosophers, on the other hand, learn less and less about more and more until finally they know nothing about everything.* Being a musician as well as a scientist, my fate, perhaps, is to end up knowing either everything about everything—or nothing at all. The jury is still out.

As a matter of fact, I find as I get older that I believe more and more in less and less. I remember reading that LDS chemist Henry Eyring's father advised him on his departure for university training in the Ivy League: "Remember, Henry, in this church we don't have to believe anything that isn't true." I have happily appropriated that remark as a personal motto. My life in the church has amounted to trying to find the eternal truths hidden in the institutional wrapping, in other words, a gradual winnowing of the wheat from the chaff, or the toys from the packaging, which is probably a more accurate statement of what that amounts to.

Perhaps the starting point was when I was in high school and really looked forward to the year when the seminary curriculum was Church History. I sincerely wanted to know some details—dates, places, the characters of the main participants, and so on—that never seemed to be given in Sunday school. I found out rather quickly that very little "history" was actually taught in Church History at seminary. What we got was the same old lessons, mostly on the Word of Wisdom and chastity (we were teenagers, after all), but with the moralistic stories drawn from church history rather than from the scriptures or conference talks. Later, I figured out why the class turned out that way: somebody in the Church Education System must have decided that the truth was too dangerous (or maybe just too raw) for teenagers. I was very disappointed, and started at that point to look at church curriculum materials with a little bit of suspicion.

Despite my hopes, even the ostensibly higher-level classes at the University of Utah's LDS Institute of Religion were only marginally better. My disappointment with the regular curriculum was only compounded when my home ward called Paul Hodson, a vice president of the university, as the Young Adult teacher. His class was intellectually stimulating, spiritually enriching, and just plain interesting. In short, it was everything that seminary and institute were not, and showed me that it is indeed possible to have a testimony and a brain at the same time. Incidentally, I often invited my girlfriend to come to that class with me. She is now my wife, Vickie Stewart Eastman, and is a long-time Sunstoner whose introduction to liberal Mormonism may have come in that very same class.

Meanwhile, across the street from the institute, I was learning the scientific method. You know how they say it works: You carefully make a hypothesis, set up an experiment to prove or disprove the hypothesis, carry out the experiment, then thoughtfully analyze the results, and repeat. In principle, the outcome is a steady increase in knowledge. Another aphorism: *In principle, principle and practice are identical; in practice, they aren't.*

After earning BA and PhD degrees in chemistry at the University of Utah, I got a job as a research chemist for Phillips 66 in Bartlesville,

Oklahoma, and started finding out just what practicing science is all about. It wasn't what I thought, nor was it what I had been taught in high school about the scientific method. Science in the real world is somewhat messier—practice differs substantially from principle. My field, in the beginning at least, was catalysis. For those of you who have always stayed as far away from chemistry as you can, a catalyst is defined as a compound that facilitates a chemical reaction without itself emerging as something different after the reaction. In practice, catalysts in the petroleum industry are sort of little synthetic rocks that you stuff into some of those big tubes you see when you drive past a refinery. Crude oil or some other fraction of the barrel is usually heated up, then run over the catalyst, sometimes with, for example, hydrogen mixed in. You then expect and hope that something good will happen. You already know what's going to happen without the catalyst: you'll make coke or road tar or some other kind of near-worthless gunk. But if you have the right catalyst, you can make gasoline out of road tar, or perhaps take the sulfur out of diesel fuel, or make gasoline from butane.

Sounds good—and it is good, and it's a lot of fun to do in the laboratory, and even more fun if something you develop ends up being really useful. The problem is that it's also very difficult. Even after about a century of research in petroleum catalysis, we still know all too little about how it really works on a molecular level, except in the simplest cases. It's still very much a trial-and-error, "I've got a good feeling about this," kind of thing. Some days, I felt as though I should have traded in my lab coat for a black robe with moons and stars on it, plus a pointed hat and a wand.

So why am I telling you all this? Well, it turns out that there can be quite a lag time between brewing up a new test catalyst in the lab and getting the results back. And, of course, you can't just wait for the results of one test before you make some more catalysts, since you have to look busy or the boss gets nervous. So you have to keep in your mind a number of different experimental directions, sometimes without knowing which ones are really going to work—but you have to act on the putative success of some of those experiments before the results are in. And, of course, the results are not always clear cut. There was a maxim in our lab that success is usually not marked by somebody shouting, "Eureka!" Instead, the eventual triumphs typically start with somebody looking at a lab book and muttering, "Gee, that's funny."

All in all, it sounds a lot like life. Most of the answers are not clear-cut, and it can be a long time after the experiment before you know what the right answer was. I believe it was Neal A. Maxwell who said that most of the big decisions in life have to be made on the basis of insufficient information. Those of us in second marriages have a fair amount to say about that particular subject.

The coping strategy developed by most scientists is pretty simple, and is right in line with the way science works. You'll remember that in science something is held to be true only until it can be shown to be false, so what we know is in some sense always tentative. The strategy then is to learn how to regard everything as true for the moment, defining truth as what agrees with experiment. That works pretty well most of the time, but it's not without problems—and the problems that arise have a lot to do with why I as a scientist can also be happy as an active Mormon.

What happens if two contradictory things are both "true," as far as we can tell? This is a situation that arises in science from time to time, but is also common when both science and faith address the same issue. Let me give an example from science: consider the case of light. For many years, light was considered to be wave-like in form and composition. It's easy to see that light can be bent or diffracted by raindrops or a prism into its separate wavelengths (colors, if you like), a discovery made by Isaac Newton in the seventeenth century. There is a well-developed body of mathematics that can beautifully describe and predict almost everything about the behavior of light as waves. In short, it is true that light can be considered to be made up of waves. On the other hand, there are some situations when light clearly acts differently, as discrete particles. For example, Robert Millikan proved Albert Einstein's postulate that the energy in a light beam, rather than being distributed through space in a wave, could be concentrated in small packets called photons. Arthur Compton proved in 1921 that a photon in collision with an electron behaves as a particle, with kinetic energy and momentum.

Is light then a wave or a particle? The best answer is probably, "Yes." With respect to light, scientists have to hold simultaneously in their minds two contradictory truths. How light has to be defined depends on how you look at it, the type of question you ask, and how you determine the answer to that question. In some situations, it's best to use one set of equations, but a completely different set must be used in other situations.

Is truth then relative, rather than absolute? Well, in science, how matter behaves is relative to the situation—and that's the absolute truth!

I find that in some ways science and religion are very much the same—what you perceive as truth depends on the questions you ask and the path you take to determine the answers to those questions. Several years ago, to the best of my memory, Stephen Jay Gould defined science and religion as what he called "non-overlapping magisteria (NOMA)," with magisterium defined as a domain where a particular form of teaching holds appropriate tools for meaningful discourse and resolution of questions. In other words, science and faith—as different magisteria—use different tools to formulate and answer questions about reality.

Though some have criticized Gould's NOMA formulation, I find it a very useful way to grasp and handle truth in whatever form it appears, from whatever source. I have spent a career trying to tease truth from Mother Nature in the laboratory and in the field, and, frankly, there are few thrills comparable to knowing that you are the first person in the history of humankind to have discovered something about the world we live in and how it works. I have also been active in the church since my youth, and have discovered that the thrill of spiritual discovery is one of those few comparable experiences.

Here's how it works for me. By and large, science is capable of answering questions of how the world works, of describing the physical, chemical, and biological processes that act in and upon our universe. To me, it is part of that wonderful process of evolution in which we believe as Latter-day Saints: that we can evolve from humanity to godhood. Science is very, very good at formulating and answering those questions—but it is not particularly good at handling questions of behavior, and of the inner, spiritual life. For those questions, the scientific method is not appropriate; in fact, it doesn't work at all. For one thing, it's difficult to design experiments to give unequivocal results about, for example, the power of prayer. There are just too many variables that one cannot constrain. Yet, in my own life, I have had experiences and felt influences that I am convinced were not the results of my own wishful thinking, but came from outside myself. I have learned by experience when the Spirit is trying to tell me something, or when I have done the right thing, even when "the right thing" was not what my own mental powers had envisioned. Unlike in the lab, I haven't been able to reproduce those things at will—but I really haven't tried. The methods of spiritual research—and the results—are quite different from those of scientific research. Yet both can elicit truth. Sometimes the results are seemingly contradictory, like light as both a particle and a wave, but I have found that each approach is useful in its place.

I remember reading an interesting talk by Truman Madsen, who, when a recent PhD graduate in philosophy, was quizzed by a student as to how he, Madsen, could still be an active Mormon. Madsen asked his interrogator a series of questions to try to uncover, not the questioner's own degree of "activity" in the church, but his level of spiritual experience, the extent to which he had participated in spiritual life, not just shown up at church meetings and activities. The key point for me was Madsen's final response to the student, which I recall as: "The difference between you and me is not so much the various enterprises we have studied or sought to master … ; the difference is that I have had some experiences that you haven't had. And that means that you are not about to leave the Church, as you say. You have never really been *in* it. He resented that and told me that he had several standard quorum awards…but I said 'No, the Church's flowing powers have not really been in you, whatever the geography of your Sunday afternoons.'" Basically, people like that student have never removed their spiritual training wheels, so they have no idea what it feels like to move along without them. But once felt, neither riding a bike nor feeling the Spirit can ever be completely forgotten.

Now, one of my personal problems with Gould's approach is that it tends to completely separate science and faith, even though I, like most people, perceive significant interaction between the two. Einstein, for example, famously noted that "science without religion is lame; religion without science is blind."

My own favorite solution to the problem is found in a discourse by Father Lehi, from 2 Nephi 2 in the Book of Mormon. *"For it must needs be that there is an opposition in all things. If not so…righteousness could not be brought to pass, neither wickedness, neither holiness nor misery, neither good nor bad. Wherefore all things must needs be a compound in one.*" I take this to mean that our lives interact with many different continua, many different value scales. For example, in the Garden of Eden, Adam and Eve were presented with the option to start confronting good and evil. That is only the first of the continua that humankind had to face. I consider these issues continua because we seldom have to deal with absolute evil or get to enjoy absolute good. There is always some mix, some place along a scale between one end of the continuum and the other, some shade of gray rather than pure black or pure white. Consider faith/works, light/darkness, male/female, knowledge/faith, sickness/health, action/contemplation, principle/practice, obedience/freedom, rest/work, and a host of others—including science/religion. At any moment we care to look, we find ourselves somewhere along each one of these continua. Our personal identity may be described as the total of all the values we exhibit for all the continua in our lives. In other words, as Lehi puts it, our lives are "a compound in one" of all those continua, all those factors. Sometimes I think it would make an interesting paper to look at all those criteria for a number of people, then do what's called a hierarchical cluster analysis of the data. That's a statistical technique designed to show how sets of data separate into identifiable groups, and what makes those groups differ from each other.

So why do I stay? Is there conflict between science and faith, both of which strongly affirm the truth of sometimes contradictory positions? Yes, indeed—but remember the wave *versus* particle discussion. The NOMA approach has allowed me to accept truth from science using one set of rules, asking one type of question to discover one set of answers, while using faith with its different set of rules and different questions to obtain a different set of answers. I find I'm not willing to give up on either methodology, because the answers I get from each one tend to be intellectually and spiritually satisfying. I've learned a lot from both methods. And, remember, we do not have to believe anything in this church that isn't true.

Is the organizational church sometimes difficult, misguided, exasperating, and just plain wrong? Absolutely! As I said at the beginning, I find I'm believing more and more in less and less. The core of the matter, the atonement of the Savior, is becoming more and more important and a lot of other things are falling away because they are so much less significant over the long run. To be completely honest, it's often difficult to reconcile what I have learned by faith and what I have learned from science. But the grand experiment is not yet over, and the boss gets nervous if he doesn't see us busy. So I guess I'll stick it out until I really know—whenever that is.

Remember my aphorism about scientists and philosophers? I think that, in the end, the Lord intends for us to combine the best of both magisteria, that our goal is—like God—to know everything about everything. It can be very frustrating as a scientist to realize how little we really know about some of the most simple things—for example, though we can write some very useful equations about gravity or attractions between elementary particles, we haven't much idea how and why those things work. Similarly, it's very frustrating as a spiritual seeker to recognize that we really don't know enough about how God works to predict when a prophecy will be fulfilled, a blessing received, or a prayer answered.

It all reminds me of a comment from the professor with whom I studied advanced thermodynamics. He said, "The first time I took thermodynamics, I hardly understood anything. The second time I took thermodynamics, I thought I understood all but a few little details. The third time I took thermodynamics, I realized I didn't understand it at all, but by then it was so useful that I couldn't do anything without it." Just like thermodynamics, I've come to realize that I don't understand spiritual things at all well—but they are so much part of me now that I refuse do to without them. And when you come right down to it, that's why I stay.

Leaving and Staying: An Interwoven, Unified Path

Gloria Pak

When it comes to church and the question of staying or leaving, I have discovered that I stay for the same reason I earlier left. By that I mean my staying and leaving seem to be merely different ways to describe the innate movement of growing up, deepening, and unfolding more fully into who I am. Zooming out, I see more and more how these seemingly disconnected, opposing directions are interwoven into a unified path.

Case in point: Even the beginning of my own spiritual roots in Mormonism was born out of a "leaving." My parents joined the church through their exodus from their native religious traditions, Buddhism and Catholicism. In addition to their spiritual heritage, they also left their homeland of Korea to come to America shortly after they were married. Watching my parents grapple with the challenges of immigrant life, I have wondered at times why they just didn't stay in Korea. But there is a part of me that knows they came here because they were eager for growth, opportunity, and even the unknown. It is the same yearning that seems to move each of us in our own time to leave our nest and enter into the wilderness, so to speak. On the surface and in the context of church, this may look like staying or leaving, but underneath the labels, I am coming to find that there is something deeply trustworthy about listening to the movement itself, regardless of the direction. This is not unlike Eve, who, upon the precipice of entering mortality or leaving Paradise, relied on her intuition to be willing to fall upward, and thus helped to open the path for all of us to choose when, where, and how we leave or stay.

My fall started around four years ago. Having been born and raised LDS, and loving my experience in the church for so many years, when church no longer felt like home, my leaving was as much a shock to me as it was to my family and friends. During this time, my vision of community was growing and a sense of what was possible on my spiritual journey was expanding. As this was happening, I became discontent with my experience at church. Some of this was related to my discomfort and frustration over the state of those within the LDS community who are misunderstood and marginalized. After a few months of this internal friction, questions about why I continued to stay became more urgent.

When I was really honest with myself, I concluded that my main reasons for staying were fear of losing my identity as a lifelong Mormon (and all the meaning I had made in that context) and fear of being judged by those around me if I did leave. Countering such fears was the assumption that perhaps it was better to stay and be part of the solution. In the face of my ambivalence, I decided to stop going to church and for the next year gave myself permission not to know what was next. This choice was the "out breath" I hadn't realized I needed. The spaciousness was rejuvenating, yet daunting and disorienting. It was during this time I learned to wean myself from acting from a place of "should." I also learned that through the deflating of my former self-identifications, there was life beyond them.

Looking back, my leaving was like a spiritual winter. It was quiet and serene, but lonely. It was full of loss and what often seemed like wandering in stretches through a barren land. Yet I was surprised to see that, by honoring the natural rhythm of this season, what followed was a season of change and renewal, a gradual willingness and even a budding desire to return to communion with my church community. When I stopped going, it wasn't with the idea of divorcing myself from the church irretrievably, but I also didn't have a specific intention or plan to come back. It was more about being honest with what was true for me in the moment and a willingness to live that truth, one moment at a time. Somewhere along that path, I came to my own embodied realization that leaving was not a permanent answer. I came to realize that the question of staying or leaving was less important than knowing that my spiritual center, the place that governed my thoughts and actions, was what was most meaningful to me.

As I have started coming back to church, I realize, paradoxically, that doing so is possible because I gave myself the space to leave. Thus the following reasons I give for staying are not meant to convince anyone else to either stay or leave. Rather, they are intended to share my perspectives on my own spiritual journey.

I stay, as I said, for the same reason I left—to grow and find spiritual nourishment. The difference is that now I'm living into a different set of questions and exploring dimensions of the divine in new ways.

One of the reasons I stay is to explore my relationship with conflict and tension. A part of me realizes that wherever I go tensions are inevitable. So I show up on Sunday, in part, to face the reality of my local congregation and neighborhood. Being in contact with my neighbors and my fellow ward members reminds me that in some ways it really isn't possible to leave. That is, the reality is that we share this earth and our humanity with others, especially those in the closest proximity to us. Whether I show up on Sunday or not doesn't change that. It also doesn't mean showing up passively. Rather, it is about not denying the reality that we live in a particular space and time, in a landscape with a community of others. And while there are plenty of problems in the world worthy of my attention, the problems of being part of a religious community are ones that I have lived through and am living through. This means I am intimate with the suffering borne by others, both distant and near, including the wounds of my neighbors, friends, and loved ones. Call it karma or fate, but my joy is intertwined with this suffering. My healing is inextricably bound to the healing of others—of the whole.

I stay to live into the question of how to integrate my roots. There is a temptation to start from scratch and leave behind all that is familiar, but that doesn't feel right. So that question burns bright. Whether it is my Korean heritage or my religious heritage, I recognize there are unique gifts in each tradition, and I am exploring how to preserve those gifts while letting go of the constructs that no longer serve us or future generations. In some circles they call this the ability to transcend and include, leaving nothing good behind as we mature. How we do this is something I feel is worthy of my attention and experimentation.

I stay because I'm learning how to translate love. In a ward family filled with so many diverse personalities and perspectives, it is easy to get lost in the words and even the content of what we are talking about. Learning to go the source from which people are speaking is an ongoing practice that stretches me. I'm glimpsing that whether we see ourselves as orthodox or progressive, the commitment to the values we hold as dear comes from a shared source. I'm discovering a ground that is deeper than I have ever known that is holding us all. I'm learning to recognize the beauty of the gesture itself. It comes from the very center of us.

Every system of language, whether it resonates with us at a particular stage of our spiritual journey or not, is the sacred home of someone. Entire lives and worlds are built upon it. Learning to honor this and be gentle when one is invited into someone's space is a continual practice. Being part of my congregation and community reveals to me ways in which my heart is still too small. All it takes is one Sunday to reveal to me the limits to my love and understanding. In increments I am hoping to hone my skill at understanding instead of habitually showing up as the one hoping to be understood.

I stay because I need practice being part of a community, a collective. Ours is a time in which it is very easy to silo ourselves into our own lives; thus, being part of the church community allows us to notice the collectives we are already a part of, including our immediate family, our neighborhood, and our spiritual community. Staying is an opportunity to make community a conscious practice. Through being a part of a group, I am able not only to enjoy the gifts of communion but to discover my own boundaries and opportunities to practice taking risks. I've found that the community itself is a wise teacher. As an intersection of perspectives, I continue to learn how to be aware of others' needs, not in spite of my own needs, but as my very own needs.

Built into the LDS cosmology is leaving home and returning to it. Rather than thinking of it as a far-off future, I like to think that home is the state of being when we can hold everything as it is and everyone as they are. In this way, I am both learning and yearning to come home.

I do not yet know what ultimately coming home will look like or whether it will involve continuing to stay within the formal Mormon praxis or being drawn elsewhere. Wherever it takes me, I hope that, like Eve, I can continue to trust that I know where I need to be to grow—in that living church to which we all belong. Regardless of where I am, my intention is to stay open-hearted, to stay aligned with my truth moment to moment, and to stay committed to listening to what is calling me and what is being called of me. That is the only place I can ever really stay.

It Is Foolish to Deny Your Heritage

H. Parker Blount

What does it mean "to stay"? If "staying" means regularly attending a two-hour service each Sunday, being available for any and all assignments, and saying, "I know this is the only true church upon the face of the earth," then, I can't say that I have stayed. If, on the other hand, staying means affirming that Mormonism has had a powerful influence on who I am, then, I have stayed.

There was a point in my life years ago when I was trying to shed some of my Southern enculturation. Someone said to me that it is foolish to deny your heritage. Since then I have learned that no matter how bewildered I may be with aspects of both my Southern and Mormon heritages, there is that mythological red thread of destiny that connects and binds me to both.

How tightly that thread binds me was revealed in an experience I had a year or so ago. My wife and I joined several other people for dinner at the home of our neighbors, Janisse Ray and Raven Waters. If you are from the South, and are at all literate, you will know Janisse Ray from her book *The Ecology of a Cracker Childhood*.[1]

Janisse, who was raised in a fundamentalist religion, and I have had many conversations about religion and the role they played in shaping our lives.

As we sat down at the table, one man, whom I had only met moments before and who had driven from a nearby town with another couple, said, "We discussed religion all the way over. We started with the Mennonites and moved on the Mormons." I immediately bristled, knowing he hadn't intended to say anything complementary. "What did you have to say about the Mormons? I'm a Mormon," I asserted. He said something to the effect about what hard-working, nice people they were. I was having none of it, and even suggested that was a polite deflection. Everyone at the table was silent, Janisse was mortified, and, sitting right beside me, whispered, "But, Parker, you don't even believe." I always thought I had a pretty good grasp of church governance and, until recently, church doctrine. I have now learned that some of what I thought was doctrine is actually folklore. I am still trying to distinguish between official and unofficial folklore.

Now, years later, I am still embarrassed, but also intrigued, about my outburst. When a friend who was also at the dinner asked me about it later, I said, "I just didn't want to listen to falsehoods about the church I don't believe in." He laughed; we both laughed. Nevertheless, my reaction is evidence that part of me still lives in the Mormon world and remains firmly connected to the LDS Church.

One way in which I stay is that the Mormonism is the one body of knowledge that I know best. I'm not saying I know all there is to know about the church, but I am saying that over the years I have formed a multitude of images, thoughts, and questions that exceeds in volume what I know about anything else.

A common Mormon aphorism is that you can leave the church, but you can't leave it alone. It doesn't matter if you characterize your testimony as a tree with deep roots and full mint green foliage or a vine with dying yellow leaves; if you have been engaged with the church for a sufficient time, there is a point where the church, as part of your psyche, doesn't leave you alone. At least daily something about the church enters into the chatter of my thoughts. There are times when I deliberately invite them in. But there are other times when I can have an idea that I wish to pursue and I sit down to make some notes about it, and the next thing I know, it has morphed into something about the church. I didn't intend to write about the church; I wanted to stay away from it, but there it comes like mist rising off the river. In that sense the church simply abides with me, is my ever present companion.

I close with a little gospel song my Mormon grandmother use to sing called "Precious Memories":

Precious memories, how they linger,
How they ever flood my soul.
In the stillness of the midnight,
Precious, sacred scenes unfold.

Notes

1. Minneapolis, Minnesota: Milkwood Editions, 1999.

Walking One Another Home: Why I Continue to Stay

Robert A. Rees

> "You can't really know a religion from the outside,
> and you can't simply 're-create' it to your liking."
> —Christian Wiman, *My Bright Abyss*

> "Going home. Going home, / I'm just going home.
> It's not far, just close by, / through an open door."
> —American folk song

At a time when many of my family and friends have left or are contemplating leaving the church (actually or emotionally), the question of why *I* stay has taken on new meaning—and has required new introspection and renewed negotiation. In my essay "I Place It in My Heart," published in the first volume of *Why I Stay* (2011), my reasons for staying were divided into three main categories: People, Principles, and Commitments. Those are still valid categories.

In regard to the first, I said, "One of the chief reasons I stay is related to people. This includes my family of origin; my siblings, my wife's siblings and their families; my children; my grandchildren; my friends; and a group of people with whom I have a tangential relationship but whose faith is somehow connected to my faith. I also stay because I believe my staying may have an influence on those in future generations who will face the question of staying."

Today, I continue to stay for all of these people, but I also stay for others, including those who lived and died before I was born whose sacrifice paved the way for the many blessings of the gospel that grace my life. My staying honors their devotion. I stay for Ruth, the woman to whom I was married for fifty-one years, whose passing in 2012 has not diminished her influence on my life. I stay for my new wife, Gloria, whose lifelong devotion to the church and gospel and whose intelligent discipleship have enriched my life immeasurably. I stay for those who have come into my circle of friendship and fellowship in the intervening years. I stay for all those whom I have taught and to whom I have borne witness of the truths of the gospel. I stay for those charged with leading the church because I feel, in spite of their occasional errors and mistakes, they need the support of people like me who see beyond their limitations to their goodness and humanity. I stay for those who will come after me who might be inspired by my devotion to something higher than myself—something as grand and glorious as the gospel of Jesus Christ, including those exciting and enlightened expansions of that gospel that have come through the Restoration. I want all of those for whom I stay to know that my faithfulness is "stronger than the cords of death" (D&C 121:44).

I also stay for specific individuals: Sister May Stanton,[1] an 85-year-old widow in my ward to whom I minister whose heart aches from family neglect; Emily Davis, one of my university students who wonders if there is a place in the church for feminists like her; Tom and Sarah Porterfield, new converts whom the bishop asked me to help with marital issues; Fred Compton, a closeted gay teenager in a neighboring ward with whom I have counseled; Sam Eliot, a former bishop in our stake who has confessed to me that he is no longer a believer; and Tim and Sally Hanks, friends who have been ostracized in their ward in Phoenix for championing gay rights.

One of the reasons I stay is because in an increasingly secular world I want to be an affirming voice for goodness and for godness, both of which I find in the Church of Jesus Christ of Latter-day Saints. I want to affirm the possibility within Mormonism of holiness and transcendence. I want to affirm the reality of God and his presence in the world, to testify that, as Alfred Lord Tennyson said, "Closer is He than breathing, and nearer than hands and feet."[2] I want to affirm the reality of Heavenly Mother, whose presence, if not always evident in the church itself, if we choose, may be so in our hearts and in our lives. I feel her love and her wish that none of us will ever feel like motherless children as long as she spreads her wings of love to envelope and embrace us.

I stay for those who have difficulty staying. I want others to know that belief is as much a choice as unbelief and that everyone believes something—even if it is nothing! In other words, belief, like unbelief and disbelief, is based not on scientific evidence, irrefutable facts, or objective reality, but rather a "propositional attitude" influenced by reason, evidence, and facts, but is also a mixture of subjective intuitions, objective possibilities, and a deep sense of heart, mind, spirit, and body coherence. In other words, we all believe in things, many core to our existence, that cannot be proven. Some saints who have full knowledge of all of the things other saints find so problematic about the gospel or the church (and which, therefore, cause them to leave the church) still find reasons to believe, still feel that staying is the best option for them.

As a person who has wrestled all of his adult life with the contradictions, perplexities, and conundra of committed devotion, I want to help those who contemplate leaving to know that staying is also a good choice, one attendant with many blessings, positive outcomes, and occasional wonderful surprises.

I stay because as a scholar and critic I have been blessed to see the church through the prism of rigorous intellectual probing, deep questioning (including of my own axioms), and broad religious and spiritual history, which have given me not only a deeper insight, but a broader perspective, a more compassionate understanding of Mormon culture, and a more imaginative hope for its future. I see the flaws and limitations of the church and its leaders, but I also see its and their potential to become better and more Christ-centered than it is and they are, just as I hope the same for myself. I stay because I want others to hope what I hope for—a more enlightened and evolved Mormonism, one focused less on being the true church and more on the search for the truth, goodness, and beauty that bless all God's children.

I stay because I want to continue working for justice and equality in the church. I stay for women—those in my own family and my many Mormon sisters who keep hoping for greater recognition, inclusion, and involvement in our church community. I want to lend my voice to their voices for women's expansive presence in the Kingdom of God. I want to continue to speak on behalf of our gay, lesbian, bisexual, transgender and intersex brothers and sisters, to champion their cause, including their desire to find love in the way that we, their heterosexual brothers and sisters, do. I believe that by staying and championing these causes, they have a greater chance of being realized.

I stay because I want to continue to try to save and serve the church's tens of thousands of malnourished children through the work my colleagues and I do on behalf of the Bountiful Children's Foundation. As I have traveled to Guatemala, Colombia, Haiti, Peru, the Philippines, Madagascar, and the South Pacific over the past decade to minister to these children, I have come to believe that they constitute one of the most compelling reason for me to stay. By staying for them and their faithful parents, I am in a better position to persuade the church and the saints in the prosperous stakes of the church to help save their lives, which requires only the smallest of sacrifices (and for most of us no a sacrifice at all). I stay because the healthy development of these children's minds and bodies will make a profound difference in the future of the church. Who knows but that today a future prophet of the church or general president of the Relief Society is malnourished and in need of help in Peru, Mongolia, or Zimbabwe? I stay because I am under covenant to regard these children as among the least of God's children, because they literally are.

I stay because I want to be an agent for peace—peace in the church and in the world. As followers of the Prince of Peace, we are under obligation, confirmed by revelation in this dispensation, to "renounce war and proclaim peace"(D&C 98:16). Further, we are told that Zion is destined to become "a land of peace, a city of refuge, a place of safety for the saints of the Most High God" (D&C 45:66). In the last pre-millennial days, we are promised that Zion will be the only place where those committed to peace and nonviolence "will not take up [their] sword[s] against [their] neighbor[s]," the only place where people can flee for safety, for those who live there will be "the only people that shall not be at war one with another" (vv. 63–69). I stay because I want to help create the conditions for such a place and such a peace, even though I may not live to see their realization.

As mentioned earlier, I stay for the leaders of the church. I am familiar with their faults and failures, some of which I know by way of painful personal experience. On the other hand, much of what I know about the church and its leaders, also through personal experience, is good and uplifting. Several years ago, I heard a podcaster characterize the church as "a Mormon Chernobyl" and at a recent symposium overheard someone speak of the general authorities as "evil," as if they were a single monolithic entity. Any person, group, or institution can be stereotypically reduced to one word, but all the words in the world are insufficient to describe a single human being, let alone a group or church.

Although our leaders should be respected and revered, their biographies should not be hagiographies. It is healthy for them as well as for the rest of us to recognize their limitations and acknowledge their fallibilities without demeaning or denigrating them. As B. H. Roberts wrote over a hundred years ago:

> The position [in his history of the church] is not assumed that the men of the New Dispensation—its prophets, apostles, presidencies, and other leaders—are without faults or infallible, rather they are treated [in this history] as men of like passions with their fellow men [and women]. ... But while the officers and members of the church possess this spiritual treasure [i.e., their charge in relation to preaching the gospel and administering the affairs of the church], they carried it in earthly vessels; and that earthliness, with their human limitations, was painfully manifested on many occasions and in various ways, both in personal conduct and in collective deportment."[3]

Sometimes leaders, local and general, say things, implement policies, and take actions that harm and injure others. Sometimes they teach things that turn out to be false. It is sobering, for example, to acknowledge that thirteen prophets, beginning with Brigham Young, and hundreds of apostles believed and taught the erroneous doctrine regarding the worthiness of Blacks to hold the priesthood and participate in temple rituals, teachings that have been disavowed by the contemporary church. Until recently, a majority of modern church leaders held incorrect ideas about the etiology and nature of homosexuality, with tragic consequences for some individual gay and lesbian saints and their families; some leaders continue to hold prejudicial views about transgendered people and negative attitudes about the equality of women.

The problem isn't in acknowledging these and other unflattering facts about the church and its leaders, it is in denying them, for the crux of the current faith crisis is not rebellion or unrighteousness, but rather a break in trust with leaders and with the church itself. Believing that church leaders are nearly infallible and will never lead us astray and that the church constitutes not only a seamless garment of revealed truth, but is "the one and only true church," many become disillusioned when they are unable to reconcile such idealization with their own discoveries, observations, and experiences. Wallace Stevens said, "The imperfect is our paradise."[4] It is so precisely because acknowledging our imperfection and that of our leaders allows us to avoid dishonesty and hypocrisy and thereby courageously face the challenge of spiritual growth and evolution, which is, after all, the purpose of the entire Plan of Salvation.

I stay an active, committed Latter-day Saint because, based on our theology, I believe my church and people have a critical, perhaps even decisive, role to play in saving this beautiful but fragile little planet spinning in space. Of all the planets in the universe, it is the only place we know of where beauty, courage, faith, imagination, grace, and love are possible. It is the only one that allows us to be human while striving for a promised existence not lower but higher than the angels. It is the only one we know where we can hear the songs of meadowlarks, watch the itinerant dance of butterflies, smell roses, swim in rivers, and wonder at the uncountable stars in the night sky. As Robinson Jeffers exclaimed, "It is only a little planet, but how beautiful it is!"

Thus, for me, there are many reasons for staying as part of what I consider my covenantal commitment not only to help build the church but to change and repair it. In an essay scheduled for publication in *Dialogue,* "Repairing the Church," I wrote,

> There is immense pain in the Church. Addressing that pain depends on our individual acts of courage, of sacrifice and especially of love. It is in that realm where much of the most important work of repairing is to be done. But there is also the larger realm, the Church beyond the individual broken heart, beyond the sin and insensitivity with which each of us must contend, beyond the madness and mystery of trying to make the gospel and the Church work in our lives, families and congregations. It is in that realm, the macrocosm of the institutional Church, where the work of repairing also is required, even though it is more daunting and more difficult

because it is largely beyond one's control. And yet it is also part of our individual and collective stewardship.

Such repairing work is to some extent consonant with the very idea of *restoration*. In an LDS general conference address, President Dieter Uchtdorf spoke of those who are inclined to "sleep through the Restoration."[5] I don't want to sleep through the Restoration or even stroll through it. Its blessings are too great and its promises too grand for me to consider doing so. The Restoration is not an event or series of events that happened in the nineteenth century; it is a process, a promise, a continual unfolding. There are many truths yet to be revealed, some of them to ordinary Saints, and I don't want to miss any of them. My guess is that not many of these "great and important things pertaining to the kingdom of God" will be revealed to those who leave the church, even though their reasons for leaving may be justified.

For me, the most unfortunate consequence of the Mormon faith crisis is not that many lose their faith in Mormonism, but that they lose their faith in faith—in religion itself and sometimes in God and Christ. Many Latter-day Saints who once testified of their love of God and of their personal relationship with the Savior no longer feel they can do so. That makes me sad.

Ultimately, I stay for our father and mother in heaven and their son because of the great gifts of creation and salvation—of being and eternal being—and of love in all of its dimensions and manifestations that their love makes possible. All of truth and goodness that I have been privileged to enjoy can be traced to those great gifts. I stay because in some small way I want to show them how grateful I am for their love. The following words of Mechthild of Magdeburg, a thirteenth-century mystic, expresses my feelings:

> Effortlessly,
> Love flows from God into man,
> Like a bird
> Who rivers the air
> Without moving her wings.
> Thus we move in His world,
> One in body and soul,
> Though outwardly separate in form.

As the Source strikes the note,
Humanity sings—
The Holy Spirit is our harpist,
And all strings
Which are touched in love
Must sound.[6]

I stay because I have faith in Latter-day Saint Christianity with its particular language, myths, symbols, ceremonies, and rituals. Christian Wiman writes,

> To have faith in a religion, any religion, is to accept at some primary level that its particular language of words and symbols says something true about reality. This doesn't mean that the words and symbols *are* reality (that's fundamentalism), nor that you will ever master those words and symbols well enough to regard reality as some fixed thing. What it does mean, though is that "you can no more be religious in general than you can speak language in general" (George Lindbeck), and that the only way to deepen your knowledge and experience of the ultimate divinity is to deepen your knowledge and experience of the all-too-temporal symbols and language of a particular religion.

Wiman adds, "At some point you have to believe that the inadequacies of the words you use will be transcended by the faith with which you use them."[7] That is, we must use language to describe and testify of our faith, but faith is something that lies beyond language, something transcendent, and, ultimately, holy. It is that quest for holiness that holds me within the circle of Christianity and Mormonism's particular expression of it.

One of the chief reasons I remain an active, committed member of the Church of Jesus Christ of Latter-day Saints is that over a lifetime I have come to trust the validity and reality of sacred spaces and the sacred experiences that are possible there. There isn't much space in the house of secularism these days for the holy, and to choose a life without holiness and all that attends it is, to quote Wallace Stevens,

> To lose sensibility, to see [only] what one sees, ...
> To hear only what one hears, one meaning alone,
> As if the paradise of meaning ceased
> To be paradise ...

... it is this to be destitute.
This is the sky divested of its fountains.

"And when the sky is divested of its fountains, ... How cold the va-
cancy ..." Stevens offers hope, however, "... in the imagination's new
beginning, ..."[8] I stay because of the promise of that new beginning,
which Christianity and the Latter-day Saint manifestation of it awakes
in my imagination.

I am now in the middle of my ninth decade. In my first decade, I
lived in a chaotic, violent, abusive, and dysfunctional world. Somehow,
by the grace of God, I survived with some sense of self intact. It was
when I was ten that I learned about God and Christ and Joseph Smith
and was baptized by my father in the font of the Mesa, Arizona, temple. As I wrote in a poem years later:

> As a boy, I too entered the water,
> baptized by my father
> raised up by my Father
> in a bowl on the backs
> of bronze oxen.
> The cereus bloomed in the night,
> blossoms of the saguaro
> scented the desert air.

Coming out of the water that day, new-born, I knew I had found a
home. Later, when I was fifteen and the only member of my family still
active, I arose early on Sunday mornings and rode the bus alone to my
church-home. Through thick and thin, through joy and heartbreak, it
has been my home ever since—and will continue to be, even if at times
I see in it similar kinds of abuse and dysfunction I experienced in my
childhood home.

In *Traveling Mercies*, Anne Lamott tells of finding her way to God
by hearing singing in a Black church, St. Andrew Presbyterian Church,
in Sausalito, California. After standing outside and listening for a number of Sundays, she slowly inched her way into the church. She writes,
"Somehow the singing wore down all the boundaries and distinctions
that kept me so isolated. [One of the songs was] so deep and raw and
pure that I could not escape. It was as if the people were singing in
between the notes, weeping and joyful at the same time, and I felt like

their voices or *something* was rocking me in its bosom, holding me like a scared kid, and I opened up to that feeling—and it washed over me." In reflecting on this experience later, she said, "When I was at the end of my rope, the people at St. Andrew tied a knot in it for me and helped me hold on. The church became my home in the old meaning of *home*—which it's where, when you show up, they have to let you in. They let me in."[9]

As I wrote in a previous essay, "That, among other things, is what churches are for—to create a home for us, to let us in. When they fail to let all of us in (including the homely, the heretics and the homosexuals), they fail in their fundamental purpose, which is to make it possible for each of us, in communion and in community, to experience the love of God and the love of others in deep, intimate ways and, therefore, to feel enough love for ourselves that we can allow the grace of God to work its miracle in our lives."[10] Someone said, we are here to walk one another home—home to our true selves, home to the community of which we are a part and home to that heavenly abode where the promise of pure, abundant, unending love awaits us. I want to be part of that journey. That's as good a reason for staying as I can imagine.

All of these are reasons I continue to stay. Together they constitute staying as a conscious and deliberate act of love. Ultimately, I feel that staying in Mormonism is the most loving thing I can do—for myself, for my family and friends, for others, and for God. I choose to stay for the possibilities and promises of what love can do.

Notes

1. The names in this paragraph are not the real names of these individuals.

2. At www.poetryfoundation.org/poems-and-poets/poems/detail/45323.

3. James R. Clark, ed., *Messages of the First Presidency of The Church of Jesus Christ of Latter-day Saints* (Salt Lake City: Deseret Book Co., 1970), 4:xiv–xv.

4. "The Poems of Our Climate," at www.immortalmuse.com/2010/06/14/tuesday-poem-the-poems-of-our-climate-by-wallace-stevens.

5. Dieter Uchtdorf, "Are You Sleeping through the Restoration?" at www.churchofjesuschrist.org/study/generalconference/2014/04/are-you-sleeping-through-the-restoration?/lang=eng.

6. At www.imere.org/content/mystical-experience-mechthild-magdeburg.

7. Christian Wiman, *My Bright Abyss: Meditation of a Modern Believer* (New York: Farrar, Straus and Giroux, 2013), 141.

8. Wallace Stevens, "Esthétique du Mal, VIII," in *The Collected Poems of Wallace Stevens,* ed. John N. Serio and Chris Beyers (New York: Vintage Books, 1954).

9. Anne Lamotte, *Travelling Mercies: Some Thoughts on Faith* (New York: Pantheon, 1999), 100.

10. "The Goodness of the Church," *Dialogue: A Journal of Mormon Thought* 41, 1 (Summer 2008): 162–73.

About the Contributors

Philip L. Barlow is a Neal A. Maxwell Senior Research Fellow and the Associate Director of the Neal A. Maxwell Institute for Religious Scholarship at Brigham Young University, Provo, Utah. Previously, he was the inaugural Leonard J. Arrington Chair of Mormon History and Culture at Utah State University, Logan. His book-length work has contemplated belief (*A Thoughtful Faith,* editor), geography (*The New Historical Atlas of Religion in America,* co-authored with Edwin Scott Gaustad), scripture (*Mormons and the Bible*), and the broader movement inaugurated by Joseph Smith (*Oxford Handbook of Mormonism,* co-edited with Terryl Givens). He has served as president of the Mormon History Association. An earlier version of his essay, "Questing and Questioning," was published in *Sunstone* magazine, November 26, 2014. He thanks *Sunstone* for permission to reprint its substance here.

Curt Bench is the owners of Benchmark Books, Inc., and, for more than forty years, has sold new, used, rare, and out-of-print books on Utah and the Mormons. He has written articles for *Dialogue: A Journal of Mormon Thought* and *Sunstone* and has published book reviews and columns in other publications. He has written historical introductions for two books on early Mormon scripture and published limited editions of several books on Mormon studies. He served for ten years on the *Dialogue* editorial board. He is a lifelong bibliophile and history lover and is an Honorary Life Member of the Utah State Historical Society. He and Pat, his tolerant wife of more than four decades, reside in Salt Lake City.

H. Parker Blount is professor emeritus of educational policy at Georgia

State University and co-author of *Educational Psychology: An Introduction*. He lives in Reidsville, Georgia.

Kathleen Cattani graduated from Brigham Young University, attended graduate school at the University of Utah, and graduated from the University of California, Hastings College of the Law. She practices employment law in Northern California. She and her husband, Mark, continue to be actively involved in their LDS ward and appreciate being a part of the community.

R. A. (Robert Alan) Christmas was loved into the LDS Church in 1957 by a sweet little gal from Provo, Utah. But he spent years as a "Jack" Mormon, and didn't sober up until he was fifty. Then he and his third wife, the late Carol Dennis, served five missions—two as actor missionaries at the Hill Cumorah Pageant with nine of their eleven kids, two in Europe (he speaks French), and one in Riverside, California. Christmas has been publishing poetry, fiction, and criticism in *BYU Studies, Dialogue: A Journal of Mormon Thought,* and *Sunstone* for over fifty years.

Alan D. Eastman grew up in Salt Lake City, served an LDS mission in France, and received a PhD in chemistry from the University of Utah. He had a successful career as a research chemist for a major oil company. He had a hard time retiring, so he co-founded a small geothermal energy company. Outside of science, he had a jazz trio for thirty-five years, and still plays keyboards in several swing bands. Just to keep in practice, he keeps the congregation's attention during hymns in his home ward (he's one of two ward organists) by changing the chords as he goes. He and wife, Vickie, are longtime Sunstoners.

Jennifer Finlayson-Fife grew up as the fifth of eight children in Burlington, Vermont. She attended Brigham Young University for a bachelor's degree in psychology and women's studies, then attended Boston College for master's and doctorate degrees in counseling psychology. She wrote her dissertation on LDS women and sexual agency. She currently runs a counseling practice helping LDS couples and individuals achieve better relationships with themselves and intimate partners. She teaches online courses and workshops to members of the church on the topics of sexuality, sexual development, self-acceptance, and achieving sexual and emotional intimacy in marriage. She and her husband, John, have three children.

Russell M. Frandsen lives in La Canada Flintridge, California. He is married to Christie Hansen. They have eleven children. He practices law professionally. Russ and Christie host the Miller–Eccles Study Group and serve on the board of the Council of Mormon Studies at Claremont Graduate University. He's the oldest player in his Saturday afternoon soccer game.

Jody England Hansen lives in Salt Lake City with her husband, Mike. She is a writer, speaker, nuanced believer, mixed-media artist, activist, and advocate for creating a world where everyone can live strong, fulfilling lives. Believing we are each on our own path on the spectrum of humanity, and all overwhelmingly loved by God, she seeks to practice this by looking for God in everyone. She loves seeing the view of Mt. Olympus from her window as she writes and works with various activist and faith groups, working to connect hearts instead of build walls.

Susan M. Hinckley is an Arizona artist and writer, and the creator of the webcomic *Gray Area*. She is a longtime exhibitor with the American Craft Council; her art has appeared in numerous books and magazines and is held in private collections across the United States. She blogs about her Mormon experience at *Latter-day Faith*, and her essays have appeared in *Exponent II* and *Sunstone* magazines.

Charles Shirō Inouye is a professor of Japanese literature and visual culture at Tufts University. He is the recipient of the Lillian and Joseph Leibner Award for Distinguished Teaching and Advising and the Japan–US Friendship Commission Prize for his translations of Izumi Kyōka. His publications include *Evanescence and Form: An Introduction to the Japanese Culture* (Palgrave, 2008) and *The End of the World, Plan B* (Greg Kofford Books, 2016). He is married to Rei Okamoto and has three children: Mie, Leif, and Kan. He is serving his fourth year as a seminary teacher in the Arlington Ward, Cambridge Massachusetts Stake.

Mitch Mayne is an openly gay, active Latter-day Saint, and from 2011 to 2013 served as the executive secretary in the bishopric (ecclesiastical leadership) of the LDS Church in San Francisco. He is a national voice on Mormon LGBT issues and promotes bridge-building between the Mormon and the LGBT communities. A special emphasis of Mayne's work is working with Mormon leadership, LGBT Church members, and families of LGBT youth to improve the health and well-being of LGBT individuals in the context of their faith. He works in corporate communication for a Fortune 100 firm and holds a master's degree in communication and media from Stanford University. He lives in San Francisco.

Gloria Pak is a first generation Korean American, a freelance graphic designer and illustrator based in Salt Lake City. She is also Creative Director of the non-profit Lower Lights School of Wisdom. She lives with her husband and collaborator, Thomas McConkie, their son, Phoenix, and their pup, Luna.

Carol Lynn Pearson is widely known for her activism on issues regarding women and LGBTQ people. She regards as very important her *The Ghost of Eternal Polygamy: Haunting the Hearts of Mormon Women and Men.* She recently published a new book of poetry: *Finding Mother God: The Missing Half of Heaven.* She has an MA in theater, is the mother of four grown children, and is an active member of the LDS Walnut Creek Second Ward in California. She may be visited at www. carollynnpearson.com

Robert A. (Bob) Rees is Director of Mormon Studies and Visiting Professor at Graduate Theological Union in Berkeley, California. Previously he taught at UCLA, UC Santa Cruz, and UC Berkeley, and was a Fulbright Professor of American Studies in the Baltics. He is the editor or co-editor of *Fifteen American Writers Before 1900* (1971), *Proving Contraries: A Collection of Writings in Honor of Eugene England* (2005), *A Reader's Book of Mormon* (2008), *Why I Stay: The Challenge of Discipleship for Contemporary Mormons* (2011), and *A New Witness to the World* (2020). He is also the author of a collection of poetry, *Waiting for Morning* (2017).

Ronda Roberts-Callister recently retired from the faculty at Utah State University, Huntsman School of Business. She is a lifelong member of the LDS Church and enjoys wrestling with interesting quesitons.

Eric Samuelsen grew up in Bloomington, Indiana, the son of an opera singer/university professor father, and an elementary school teacher mother, which helps explain his passion for words, music, and theatre. He earned his bachelor's degree in Theatre and Media Arts from Brigham Young University, followed by a PhD in Theatre History from Indiana University. He taught briefly at Indiana University and Wright State University before joining the BYU faculty in 1992. When illness forced him into early retirement from BYU, he began a prolific partnership with Plan-B Theatre Company in Salt Lake City, which continued until his death in September 2019.

Camilla Miner Smith grew up on a dairy farm in Sandy, Utah, and graduated from Brigham Young University with a degree in English. After graduation, she worked as an editor in Washington, DC, and in New York City, where she met her husband, George Smith, in Manhattan's Central Park. She earned an MA in English from Teachers College, Columbia University. After graduating, she taught English as a second language to Spanish-speaking welfare recipients in the South Bronx after which she and George moved to San Francisco, where she wrote and edited for the Japanese American Citizens League. Camilla currently edits the *Bancroftiana,* the newsletter for the UC Berkeley Bancroft Library's Special Collections. She does volunteer work with educational institutions, especially in music and science. And she loves interfaith work because it is so illuminating to understand what people hold dear with such fervor. The Smiths have one daughter and four sons, two of whom are identical twins. She adores each of her twelve grandchildren.

Kimberly Applewhite Teitter is a daughter, sister, wife, mother, healer, ally, and friend. She is a North Carolina native who currently resides in Salt Lake City, Utah, by way of New York City and Cambridge, Massachusetts. She is a psychologist by day and assistant director of Debra Bonner Unity Gospel Choir by night.

Emma Lou Warner Thayne wrote fourteen books of fiction, non-fiction, and poetry, including the words to the hymn "Where Can I Turn for Peace?" For thirty years, she taught English and writing at the University of Utah. She served on many academic, religious, arts, and civic boards of directors; for seventeen years was the only woman on the board of the *Deseret News;* and for six years was on the LDS General Board of the Young Women. Her last book *The Place of Knowing, A Spiritual Autobiography* was published in 2011. Emma Lou passed away in late 2014, but her legacy of bridging differences of faith and cultures lives on through her writing.

Dan Wotherspoon, PhD, is the former editor of *Sunstone* magazine and executive director of the Sunstone Education Foundation (2001–08). He is a freelance editor and public voice on issues in Mormonism, hosting the *Mormon Matters* (2011–19) and *Latter-day Faith* podcasts (2019–current). Among other works, he is the editor of the book *The Challenge of Honesty: Essays for Latter-day Saints,* by Frances Lee Menlove (2013) and is currently completing his own book, *Give Your Gifts Again: Enjoying Church after a Shift of Faith.*

How meaningful is your Mormonism?
Keeping it real. Keeping it thoughtful.

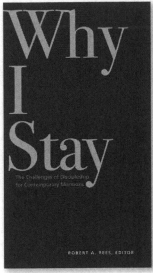

Why I Stay
The Challenges of Discipleship for Contemporary Mormons (volume 1)
edited by Robert A. Rees
hardback: $24.95 | ebook: $6.00

The Challenge of Honesty
Essays for Latter-day Saints by Frances Lee Menlove
edited by Dan Wotherspoon
hardback: $26.95 | ebook: $9.99

Mercy without End
Toward a More Inclusive Church
essays by Lavina Fielding Anderson
paperback: $18.95 | ebook: $9.99

www.signaturebooks.com